MURD SE

Murder and the Golf Course

Tales of a Leicestershire Detective

Simon Shuttleworth

YOUCAXTON
PUBLICATIONS

ISBN 978-1-914424-12-0
Published by YouCaxton Publications 2021
YCBN: 01

YouCaxton Publications
www.youcaxton.co.uk

To my Dad, Tom.

You always had a book in your hand.
I wish you could have read this one.

Preface

YOU KNOW that difficult moment in the book shop when you are trying to decide whether to buy the book in your hand? You look at the opening pages and you have to make up your mind. Shall I or shan't I?

Well, if you have got this far, stick with it.

I suppose I should be honest though.

If you like golf and you like murder investigation stories, I think you will like this book.

If, however, you take your golf *really seriously*, you are not keen on true crime stories and you break out in a rash whenever someone says '*fuck*', then maybe you should get *Life Swings by Sir Nick Faldo* and forget this one.

This is not the autobiography of a police officer. My vanity does not extend so far as to think that you want to know about my primary school adventures or read chapter and verse on a life on the beat. It *does* cover the most significant, traumatic, high profile and disturbing investigations I have been a part of.

Neither is this actually a golf book. People who write golf books can generally play the game. I know *how* to play the game; I know most of the rules and I usually wear the right kind of clothing. But as a great comedian might once have said, '*I hit all the right balls, just not necessarily in the right direction.*'

I was talked into organising a golf trip in 1998 and this somehow became *twenty golf trips.* Some outstanding golf was played but that was never what it was about.

This dictionary entry perhaps sums it up best:

Golf *n* a game, the object of which is to strike a ball with a club into holes, usually eighteen.

Trip *n* a journey, usually involving an outward and return journey for a specific purpose.

Golf Trip *n* an event involving the drinking of an inordinate amount of beer, visits to casinos, highly dangerous swimming, fires on piers and in restaurants, Prince Charles, Chubby Brown, Dr Who, horse racing, thieving landlords, after dinner speeches, naked dancing, broken windows, unrequited love, Karaoke, Leeds United, rancid chickens, getting caught in the ladies changing rooms and Eddie, on his bugle or in his pants. Oh, and some actual *golf* (see above).

As I said though, this book is also about something else that repeatedly took me away from my family, especially in the last six years of my career.

Something much more important.

Murder investigation.

A '*187*' in the world of Michael Connelly's legendary detective, *Harry Bosch*. Thankfully, I was somewhat better at that than I was at golf, although not as good as Bosch. Hopefully, I did always follow his motto: Everybody counts or nobody counts.

I have shared the true stories of those investigations in these pages and added a few more thoughts as they have occurred to me.

In the editing stage of this book the question was raised as to how the comedy of the golf trips and some of the dafter policing incidents sits with the serious and emotive subject of murder. It is a really good question and one to which I am not sure I have the answer.

Police officers are often said to need a dark humour to help them through the tougher times. I certainly believe that. Most importantly though, I hope that those affected by the crimes I have described, feel that they got to know me well enough to realise that I cared and would never intentionally upset them.

Where necessary, to protect the innocent, the oh so guilty and my bank account, pseudonyms have been used. Some dialogue has been reconstructed to improve the flow, using a few available sources and my memory. Any errors are mine and mine alone.

Murder and the Golf Course.
Simon Shuttleworth,
East Devon, April 2021.

Contents

North West Leicestershire, 6pm, Wednesday 19th November 2015

AS SOON as we arrived in Ibstock, we got the first update. Beadman was talking to them. Kayleigh was not in Sence Valley Forest Park. According to him she was in fields on the opposite side of the road. He was saying the location was a good way into those fields and in deep undergrowth, in a hedge.

It was pitch black and raining heavily. Paul and I started walking diagonally into the fields away from the direction of Sence Valley. After about half a mile we came to some kind of a track overgrown with bushes and brambles. We could see on a phone mapping app that it was a discontinued rail track called the Blackberry Line. It looked as though there was still a bridge on the line, about 200 metres over to our right, which dissected a large pond. We headed that way.

Paul made a call and we arranged for Steve and Karen to get Beadman to mark on a map where he thought Kayleigh was. This was then compared to the tracking signal in Paul's airwave radio. While we waited for them to get back to us, we walked onto the bridge. Paul's phone rang and as he answered it, I followed him.

At one point I saw him step to the side and his free hand briefly flicked out and pointed down. About a second before I would have fallen forty feet to my death, I saw that he was pointing to a massive hole under which was nothing and then just black water.

'What the fuck was that?!' I said, 'The international hand signal for watch out there's a great big hole and you might die?'

He just looked at me and I heard him say something about detectives and shake his head.

For about an hour we tried to figure out where Steve and Karen were directing us but it became clear that the map they were using was not how the field looked in the present. We had decent torches and dragon lights but they were starting to fade.

At one point someone decided to send X-Ray Five-Five, the air support unit, overhead. It was immediately clear that the glare of their spotlights just made things worse on the canopy of trees we were in and around. I should have told them to leave straight away but we let them have a good look. Was there still some part of me thinking, 'what if she's still alive? Maybe their thermal imaging cameras will pick up her body heat?' I don't think that's the case but perhaps, subconsciously, it crossed my mind.

Sometime between 8pm and 9pm we were joined by Emma and Steve. They had fresh torches. By now we were being told that Beadman was claiming that Kayleigh had hit him with a brick and he had then thrown it at her head, killing her.

By 9.45pm we had found nothing. The four of us moved into a group to speak. It was chucking it down with rain, it was dark and cold. We agreed that there was no point recalling the search teams until it was light the next day. But we also agreed that we four, could not stop. We needed to carry on regardless.

Twenty-Eight Years Earlier

I JOINED Leicestershire Police in October 1987. The first person I went out with after graduating from training college was Ian - a tall skinny lad who was so crisply turned out he probably ironed his pants.

He showed me how to deal with rudimentary offences such as cycling on the pavement. This consisted of him driving the police van alongside someone who was cycling on the pavement, telling me to lower my window and then shouting across me '*Get off the fucking path!!*'

Ian and I were quite different at work. He was mainly better at stuff than me but only one of us was ever going to be in the CID. Ian's idea of interviewing was to shout at the prisoner until they coughed the job or started crying. Sometimes it even worked.

On my first day with him we arrested a cross-eyed man called Malcolm who had been trying to cash a stolen cheque at the Alliance and Leicester Building Society. Ian shouted at him. He wouldn't admit it, so Ian shouted a bit louder. I can't remember if we ever charged him. He looked like a man who had been shouted at before.

Unlike Ian, I was to become a detective although I did get plenty of uniformed experience first and they even let me carry a gun for a while. By 1997 I had been fully promoted to sergeant for over a year and was in charge of a small team at a police station in the city or Central Area as it was then known.

One day a Detective Constable called Alan approached me. I had got to know him a bit since my promotion but we were not friends particularly.

'*I understand you organised a golf trip to Leeds last week*' he said.

'*I wouldn't call it a golf trip but yes, a few of us had an overnighter in Leeds and a couple of rounds at Oulton Park*' I replied.

'*Well, we need a new trip for this nick so you can sort that, can't you?*'

And so, the following year, a raiding party of twelve cops descended on Whitby on the North East coast of England, for the inaugural *Central Area Golf Trip.*

Alan and I are the only two people to have gone on all twenty trips but many of them featured long-term regulars including Blackie, Jamie, Lee, Baras, Jason, the unique Eddie and the exceptionally loud Major.

As the trips began I hadn't really made my mind up what I wanted to do, long-term. For a while I thought I'd like to be a full time firearms officer but, whilst I wasn't the worst shot on the range, I was a long, long way from the best and also I failed the advanced driving test, a pre-requisite to be a firearms officer, so that was a non-starter.

Detective work and being a CID aide on the Braunstone Estate in Leicester, gave me a buzz.

Performing an armed stop on a supposed car full of armed travellers only to find inside two pregnant women telling me to '*fuck off*' when I pointed my carbine at them, not so much.

Passing the sergeants exam in 1994, at the same time I passed an interview for a full-time CID post, took me more in the direction of uniform and it was 1999 before I got a proper crack at being a Detective Sergeant.

I was involved in a lot of serious crime investigation after that, including murder. I was the Officer in the Case (OIC) as a DS, on the killing of a woman by her grown-up son. He removed her head with a Bosch chainsaw, having tried a few other models out on legs of lamb he bought at his local butcher. More of that one later.

In 2003 I was made OIC on the job that was to be one of a few that consumed my attention above everything else going on in my personal and professional life. This one wasn't a murder; it was actually the *attempted* murder of a police officer from my own station.

The perpetrator in that case, bizarre as this may be, was someone I got on with and found to be a reasonable person to talk to, despite the horrendous thing he tried to do.

Later, in 2006, when I finally made it to the Leicestershire Major Crime Unit, I was involved in many more murder investigations and I knew that I had found my niche. I never had before and have never had since, the buzz of the jury coming back to deliver a verdict on a person who has taken a life.

It is the ultimate responsibility in the life of a detective.

I left it all behind to seek further promotion but on becoming an inspector in 2007 there was only one place I wanted to be and that was right back in Major Crime, as a Senior Investigating Officer (SIO) or Deputy SIO, dealing with murder.

In 2012 I made it and although I ended up running several investigations as SIO, the three that really consumed me were all ones in which I was *Deputy SIO*, albeit with plenty of latitude to run the show a lot of the time.

More of all that later too. Back to Whitby and that first Central Area Golf Trip.

Whitby 1998

FOR THE inaugural trip, only five of us went up for the first night. The other seven came along the next morning. Whitby was recommended by one of the patrol officers at Hinckley Road, Maurice. He knew the course well because he had friends in the area. And he promptly pissed off to stay with them, rather than the shit hole he had suggested the rest of us stay in.

He had assured us that we would be OK for the night out though. Lots of good pubs doing great food and a cracking nightclub, he said. In reality there was bugger all to eat but haddock and the nightclub had closed three months earlier. Maurice wasn't asked his opinion again.

Our so called '*hotel*' was at best a couple of grubby floors of rooms above a pub. I travelled up with Jason, a Bamber Bridge lad who has been on most of the trips since. Alan was accompanied by Rich, an impressionable and easily led DC from his office. They hit the highs of Whitby a good couple of hours ahead of our 6pm arrival. Rich was already half cut when we met up.

We checked in and an early recon established that we had six rooms on the two floors for the total twelve players, the balance of which were due to arrive in time for tee off the following morning. An early worry given that we intended to sink a few sharpeners and follow up with a curry, was that we could find only one bog roll between the two toilets that we were all supposed to share.

Making a mental note to get some more toilet paper as cheaply as possible, we headed out for a few beers, although Rich was looking increasingly like a few more was not the best idea for him. We managed to get a round in each before we landed in the one and only local Indian restaurant.

Three of us were relaxed and jolly but in control. Rich was arseholed. He decided he would solve our earlier problem and proceeded into the toilets. He didn't share his plan with the rest of us.

A few minutes later, out he came trying manfully to hide the obvious. He was carrying a toilet roll. He sat down, looking from side to side like an enemy agent behind the lines.

'Rich' said Alan. *'Everyone in here knows you've got a bog roll under the table.'*

'Bugger it then' he replied. Upon which he plonked the roll down on top of the ornament in the middle of the table, proudly positioned for all to see.

Sadly, Rich was the only one who *didn't* know that there was a lit candle in the middle of the ornament and within seconds the bog roll was ablaze.

One of us, not Alan who was helpless by this time, knocked it to the floor and a plucky waiter ran over and stamped on it till the flames went out.

Most of the other customers were looking at us. Not many were laughing. Alan was on the floor. I was starting to think this was the beginning of the end for golf trips when up came the manager to make it even worse.

'I'm calling the police' he said.

No, don't call the police I thought.

Thinking quickly, I proffered a few pound coins as purchase and damages for the charred roll and presently the manager and everyone else calmed down. It had to be me. Alan was still in hysterics; Rich was totally wankered and Jason is from the North West and doesn't part with cash easily.

By the time we finished our meal we were best friends with the staff and on departure they presented Rich with a new toilet roll. He was of course, swiftly relieved of it.

Back in the hotel the pub shut much earlier than anticipated and we turned in, a bit merry but ok really. I was sharing a room with Jason and it was probably only a couple of hours before nature awoke me. That's when I found I couldn't get out of the room.

'Jase I can't get out of the room! Jase! Are you awake?'

'I am now. What?'

'I can't open the door and I am busting for a slash.'

'I know, I think Alan's done something to it. I pissed in the sink.'

I wasn't doing that so I forced the door open by giving it a good kick, fortunately managing it without doing any damage. Needless to say, Alan got a wakeup call shortly after I had emptied my bladder. He's lucky it wasn't before.

The rest of the boys, those who couldn't get their passes stamped by their partners for two nights away, turned up bright and early in time for an 8am tee off. We played *Texas Scramble*, a team game where everyone in each team hits a ball and then they all decide between them which was the best shot. Each player then then plays his or her second shot from that place and so on until the ball is in the hole. Effectively three or four people play as though they are one person. In theory a team should come out with a good score but that is not always the case.

During this round I had the pleasure of carrying Alan's bag for half a hole in a routine that was to become oh so familiar to his playing partners when he had been up late drinking beer and eating curry, the night before.

'Look after my clubs Shutts,' he shouted as we walked up a hole towards the end of the front nine. Pausing to chip a wedge beautifully into the centre of the green, which was up the hill in front of us, he then he dashed up to and through the door of the White House, an on-course hotel, to have a desperate and only just in time, shit.

He came out not looking that much more comfortable and as I have said this was to become a bit of a habit. That story in itself is pretty grim but just to make it worse I could invite you, before I mention the other times, to wonder just how often there would be a real toilet available, halfway round your average golf course.

In the afternoon we ran a *Stableford* competition, an individual event where players score one point for a bogey, two for a par, three for a birdie and so on. I didn't really trouble the 'and so on' part of that sentence much. Or ever.

Maurice had reappeared after a lovely night's sleep at his friend's place. Playing off his genuine three handicap, he scored a stunning three under par sixty-seven which began with birdie, birdie, eagle.

One of the other guys who came on a lot of trips was PD. He, like Maurice, was a uniformed Hinckley Road cop and a tremendous golfer. He played off four or five but could par a course when he was playing well.

PD was on my shift at Hinckley Road and was quite an intense character at times. At heart though, he was a kind person who entertained lots of us many times at his home club of Whetstone. Like many players of that standard, he was good for the game of us lesser mortals and he would often get me scoring twenty-five points instead of a whole lot less with a tip or an adjustment to my game.

That said, the kindness went out of the window and turned into rank bitterness and hatred towards anyone he suspected of either golf handicap gamesmanship or even worse, proper cheating.

Beating someone over the head with a bat; sleeping with your best mate's wife; stealing the crown jewels. All of these would be committed by a person of better and greater character than a golf cheat, according to PD.

On one trip he was heard to cheer out loud as Jason, playing off a handicap of twenty-one when PD thought it should have been sixteen, hooked his eighteenth tee shot into trees to squander the overall tournament lead and the title. I didn't put them out together again after that.

The thing that really rankled with PD though, was that *he thought* Maurice was a cheat. He claimed to have seen him at it on more than one occasion in club matches and in Whitby he was exceptionally vocal about Maurice's sixty-seven. Possibly slightly the more so because he came second.

On this occasion I managed to calm him down because I was playing with Maurice when he did it and I saw him go four under par after the first three holes with my own eyes. He did not cheat. He didn't have to. The eagle was a hole out from about 150 yards, pure fluke. Then he stuck it out with a brilliant one over par across the remaining fifteen holes.

His forty something Stableford score was obviously enough to take the first ever Central Golf Trip title and when I got round to buying a trophy two or three years later, his name finally got recorded there, with or without the approval of PD.

We didn't have a bad second night out in a couple of reasonable pubs but as I have mentioned, the nightclub was non-existent, so we were heading for bed by around midnight.

What I forgot to mention before was that those of us who had stayed the first night in the crummy hotel had woken up to find the kitchen out of service for breakfast. Now, we had agreed £18 per person per night for B&B in this dump and we wanted our bacon and eggs.

The manager pointed us in the direction of a decent café only fifty yards or so away and I am happy to say we got a nice full English with tea for a fiver. We were happy to pay, safe in the knowledge that it would be coming off our £18 for the first night. So imagine my surprise when paying the bill the next morning, to find that the manager was only willing to credit us £2 each for the breakfasts he had not provided.

'That's not right,' I said to this weaselly-looking individual.

'You told us which café to try, we paid a fiver for breakfast, your B & B rate is £18; £18 minus £5 is £13. You have over charged us.'

I was paying for the whole group by cheque so wrote him one out for the right amount.

I passed it over but he wouldn't take it.

'No' he said. *'I refuse to accept that. It's £12 short.'*

'Well, you can refuse what you like mate but it's all you are getting,' I said.

At which he shouted over his shoulder, in the direction of the now functioning kitchen, *'Brian!'*

Brian was the chef and he appeared, as in all classic old films, holding a big meat cleaver. Just as he did this one of the more aggressive members of the group appeared at my side, having heard most of the conversation.

His contribution was thus: *'Brian, it's your call but you can either try to do something with that knife or clear off back into the kitchen.'*

Brian promptly took the advice and disappeared. Much to the manager's dismay he was forced to meekly take the cheque or get nothing.

His parting shot was rather strange though.

'Shuttleworth', he said *'I know you. You come to Whitby for your fishing trip every September don't you?'*

'No,' I replied. *'I don't fish. It's as boring as you. Is that all?'*

'You can't fool me' he said. *'There aren't many Shuttleworths' about. I know it's you! Well I'm telling you now; you won't get a room in my town. You'll be barred from Whitby. I'll see to it!'*

'OK Wyatt Earp' I said. *'I'll leave that one with you.'*

We loaded the bags and set off for the course and the Friday casual round, before heading home. As we went, I couldn't help wondering if later in the year, poor Mr Shuttleworth the fisherman, experienced a less than friendly welcome from the seasiders of Whitby.

Skegness 1999

PROFESSIONALLY THIS was the year that I finally got the chance to move to a Detective Sergeant role at Charles Street Police Station in the city centre. I had been on the periphery of murder investigations at Braunstone but active, frequent involvement in homicide was still a few years away for me.

My introduction to death on a large scale had happened long before this, on the evening of Sunday 8th January 1989. I was still in my two-year probation period when I found myself wedged into the back of a police van, racing to East Midlands Airport on that cold night.

The Kegworth Air Disaster had just happened.

A British Midland Boeing 737 passenger jet was en-route from Heathrow Airport to Belfast when a fan blade broke in the port engine. The pilots were confused by the manner in which this affected the ventilation system. This caused them to believe that the faulty engine was to starboard and it was this one that they immediately shut down. The aircraft smashed into an embankment between the M1 and East Midlands Airport.

The pilots realised what had happened and they so nearly made it to safety. The fine margins in this kind of situation are what separates the forgotten names of the crew on Flight BD92 from heroes like Chesley 'Sully' Sullenberger who landed US Air Flight 1549 on the Hudson River in 2009.

Once we had raced up to the airport we did absolutely bugger all for what seemed like ages before being put on traffic control duties on the miles of backlogged roads, where members of the public listening to their radios gave us updates and snacks. No iPhones then.

After a few hours, things got a bit more organised and I was despatched to the airport fire station with two other junior officers. A large group of more experienced officers from my team were sent to the Thistle Hotel next the airport entrance.

The plan was that the experienced officers would speak to the arriving relatives of people thought to have been on the plane. These officers would call the three of us with names and descriptions and we would go to a nearby snow shed where the bodies pulled from the wreckage were being taken and laid out in body bags.

Our task was to try to find the described individuals. It was a gory job and one of our number quickly threw up outside.

At one point two of us disturbed a journalist from a national newspaper trying to sneak into the snow shed. We were disgusted and back then, quite naïve as to the workings of the media. My colleague, a handy lad, was all for giving this guy a kicking but common sense prevailed and we settled for sending him packing.

We dined on aircraft meals, worked ourselves to exhaustion and actually got forgotten by the relief planners so we didn't get stood down until 5pm the following afternoon. On the way back, crammed into our van again the shift inspector ordered a stop at a local off licence where he bought a couple of bottles of whisky. These were shared out in the canteen on our return before we were allowed to go. That was counselling 1980s style but hey, at least he cared.

My big introduction to death had little effect on me. I recall stories that a Leicestershire officer was sacked for trying to steal a life jacket from the wreckage. I don't know the full facts of that though. Some others received counselling for the trauma of what they had to deal with. Personally, I felt false comparing myself to survivors or their families and announcing that it had stressed *me* out.

I was twenty-two at the time and I came to realise, with maturity and experience, that colleagues could become genuinely and seriously ill from their involvement in such incidents. I guess I was one of the lucky ones.

Meanwhile the golf trips continued....

An improvement in accommodation was the obvious first thought for me and Alan as we pulled up outside the hotel in Skegness. Once we got inside and met the landlady it was more like an episode of Porridge. None of this, none of that, no bringing girls back, no one gets in after midnight blah blah blah.

Little did we know then that it was her useless husband who was to cause us what little grief we did have on this trip. He was a six-foot fat lad and he fancied himself as a hard man but he was in fact, *just a twat.*

First, we had to address the Norm issue. Norm, not his real name, was related to Jason. We called him Norm after Norman Wisdom because he was extremely comical in his movements. He was also that rarest of things, a golfer who was substantially worse than me.

The problem he presented us with was that as he arrived with Jason, his face was painted as though he was a Tiger. You know the sort of thing six-year olds get done at the fair. It was for a charity event at work apparently and he thought it would be fun to come out with us looking like that in Skegness in the middle of summer.

'*Norm, you're not mate. You'll get stabbed.*' Said some wise counsel. He washed it off.

As our first evening of beer progressed, we befriended the barman at the hotel. He was only about eighteen and seemed to know '*what was what*' entertainment wise in the town. It is hard to recall it now but back then I was thirty-three and staying up until the wee hours was a normal night.

It is only later in your fifties where you stand in the queue to the packed club wondering if you will get a seat inside. And you thank the bouncer who will not let you in because back home you are on the last couple of chapters of a really good book.

We had a few beers in the hotel and a couple of games of pool were played out between the eighteen of us who had made trip number two. Everyone was on board for two nights this time. I didn't give anyone an option to do anything else.Time ticked on and just as we were thinking it was time to make a move into Skeg itself, the young barman approached us.

He looked at Alan and said, '*Did you know the gaffer has got your ID card?*'

Alan looked blank.

'*Your ID card.......... warrant card, do you call it?*' said the lad.

Light dawned and Alan looked in his wallet. Sure enough his police warrant card was missing from its slot.

The young barman continued, '*When you paid for a round you put it on the bar with the card showing and he whipped it out.*'

At this, Alan walked over to the bar and beckoned the landlord over. He swaggered towards us but as he got within reach Alan pulled himself up onto the bar and reached over it, grabbing the idiot by the scruff of his shirt. He was a big bloke but Alan's not small and he had the momentum. The twat was pulled up over the bar.

'*I understand you've got something that belongs to me*' said Alan.

'*Let go of me, I don't know what you're on about. You're all fuckin barred,*' he bleated

'*My warrant card you thieving idiot. Or shall we make it official. Up to you.*'

Alan released him and he produced the card and then tried to mumble some more nonsense about barring us. Unsurprisingly, his argument was pooh-poohed and at the mention of involving his good lady, he decided he was off to bed with a headache.

We had a half reasonable night in Skegness itself, getting split into a couple of groups and about 1am, I decided I would turn in. The thing with organising these trips is that I have to be in good shape the next morning to sort out the tees for the Texas Scramble, dish out the water and get players off at the allotted time. I do give out team sheets beforehand but by and large people forget them.

Unfortunately for me I was sharing a room with Alan and I was woken around 3am when he came crashing in and collapsed in a heap onto his bed. Sometime after this, I am guessing around 5.30, I was woken again by him making a noise in the bathroom. I could hear running water and cursing as I looked up to see him staggering out of the bathroom dressed only in boxer shorts.

'*How do you get out of here Shutts?*' he asked.

'*What?*'

'How do you get out of here? Fuckin place.'

'Through the door' I replied, pointing at it.

He didn't really seem to be acknowledging me but he did teeter towards the door before asking the same question again a couple of times. It was then that I recalled seeing or reading something about sleepwalkers not responding to people properly and I was genuinely going to do something about it but before I could, he was gone, out of the door in his shreddies. *Should I go after him? Oh, he'll be ok.* I went into the bathroom, turned off the running tap, flushed something disgusting away that was looking up at me from the toilet pan and got a welcome couple of hours extra sleep. Lovely.

I was just about dressed in my golfing attire for the day's competition the next morning when the door opened and in walked Alan.

'What's occurring son? I just woke up in a double bed in room eight'

At breakfast, two of the lads, Phil and Ben, reported that they had heard a loud knocking at their door around 6am. Phil got up and answered it only to find Alan standing there. He told Phil to *"fuck off"* and walked away down the corridor.

It was a lovely hot sunny day and the golf at Skegness's difficult links course, Seacroft, was hard going but hey, it's a lot nicer than playing in rain. The year was a bit of a mixed up one for the format we played but Jason was declared the overall winner and his name adorns the trophy for 1999.

Alan's excesses caught up with him once more out on the course. I was again playing in the same group as him when on the approach to a green he said, *'Hold on a minute Shutts'*, paused and pinged a seventy yarder to a few feet from the pin.

'Take my clubs up mate' he said and of course this time I was fully trained and knew what to do. What I didn't expect was that he then stopped at Jason's bag to grab a bog roll Jason was for some reason carrying. Armed with that he disappeared into some bushes just to the side of the next tee.

All we could hear from that point on was *'Ow! Ow! Bollocks ow!'*

A few moments later he reappeared pulling on his shirt and doing up his trousers.

'That was a messy one' he said. *'Good job I stripped off. I didn't realise it was a gorse bush though.'*

That night we enjoyed one of the best trip nights out. The beach bar was staffed by bikini clad girls and most of us got more than merry before making our way to a club knocking out £1 bottles of beer.

The club entrance was down a flight of steep steps - probably about the size of a normal household staircase. Two of our number, Jon an ex-Royal Marine Commando and Phil who had been a Scots Guard I think, had been arguing about which was the best regiment.

On arrival at the steps, Phil announced that touching any of the steps on the way down was forbidden. He invited me to go first and I promptly slid - not too gracefully - down the banister. Jon went next and performed a much more elegant version of my method.

Phil then invited us to stand back while he jumped the lot and demonstrated a para roll at the bottom. He promptly twisted his ankle and limped round the course on the second day with it very badly swollen and strapped up. Andy McNab he is not.

About 2.30am, five of us were outside the club, standing in what had suddenly become an almost deserted Skegness town centre. As I write I am trying to piece together who was there with me. Jon was certainly one and a mate who had come as a caddy for him, Guy, was another. Alan was one of the remaining two but I can't remember the fifth.

I only know there were five of us before we lost Jon and when the burger man outside the club started packing up and giving burgers away, we had two each but ended up chucking Jon's away.

A short time later, after an unsuccessful search for Jon, we arrived back in the hotel only to find the bar closed. Guy decided he would open it and served up four cheeky pints as we racked the pool table up.

Suddenly the landlord appeared, shouting.

'Right that's theft, I'm calling the police!'

One of us pointed to the money we had already placed on the bar. Explaining the dishonesty part of the definition of theft to this moron would take some time.

He was treated to a few expletives, so I called time on the lads and they all headed up the stairs. I turned back to him and said, *'Right, time for me and you to have a word about what is happening and not happening here.'*

He thought otherwise and scuttled off back under his stone. We never saw him again.

The next morning Jon, our ex-commando, was at pains to dress us down for abandoning him in Skegness town centre whilst he had gone for a leak. He had walked back the mile or so to the hotel and finding himself locked out under the landlady's curfew order, had managed to find a way in through an unlocked first floor window.

That is the kind of training that makes our armed forces the best in the world.

Leeds 2000

THE NADIR in accommodation was reached in Leeds, shading the award by a nose from the dump in Whitby. I decided we would go and play the public but excellent Oulton Park Course between Leeds and Wakefield that I had visited in 1997, inadvertently inspiring the Central Area Golf Trip itself.

I looked at the potential for cheap accommodation and it being a golf trip I booked a place based purely on its name, The Albatross.We were back to multi-occupancy rooms and I shared and travelled with Darren, a first timer and Ben, a mate who later left Leicestershire to become a Devon and Cornwall detective.

The Albatross was opposite some kind of estate with blocks of flats on it. The bar was full of all kinds of weird and wonderful previously unheard of brands of drink like *Leopard* bitter and *Hawk* Lager.

The rooms were on the first floor and they left something to be desired. At the time I was suffering with a back injury and had to do some exercises in the morning to loosen up. This involved lying on my back and doing hamstring stretches and the like. There was no way I was doing that in front of piss-taking mates so I decided I would do it in the bathroom.

In the end I had to wait until I had showered so I could lay my towel on the minging carpet to do this. You would not have wanted to de-flea your dog in the place.

Downstairs at breakfast time the landlord did the fry-ups with a fag on, asking individuals if they wanted one egg or two as he flicked ash out of the way over the frying pan. Some would say it was character building. I imagine it put hairs on your chest too.

The main golfing day was not one of the more memorable ones. That is my quick way of saying I can't remember much about it. Apart from, in the afternoon, during the tournament proper, it pissed down. It started raining for my group on the third tee.

Jon and I had a caddy each. No expertise involved, just two extra lads who wanted to come on the trip but didn't want to play golf. Jon's caddy was Greg. He lasted until the hole after the rain started before announcing to the group, '*Sod this, I'm off*,' and went to the pub.

My caddy Roscoe took it much more seriously and to my embarrassment, especially as I am hardly Nick Faldo, he insisted on doing everything for me. He dried my clubs and in the torrential rain held the brolly over my head, at his own expense, until I was ready to take my shot. It is probably what propped me up off the bottom of the pack by a few places as well.

On about the fifteenth hole we had the longest drive competition. This is a hole, usually a longish par five, on which a player wins a prize for hitting the ball the longest distance, provided the ball is on the fairway. If it runs off the short stuff and into the rough it does not count. With a long standing dodgy back and three quarters of a back swing, this is not something I usually trouble the scoreboard with. This time, we decided no-one was looking and we could let Roscoe have a go. He deserved it after all his effort. I wasn't quite banking on him hitting the ball further than me but you live and learn. Bloody caddies.

The rain stopped for us on the seventeenth green and on the eighteenth tee I hit my best shot of the round. Straight as a die, the ball flew up the middle of the fairway just over a ridge, smack in line with the green. If only I had been able to find it when I got up there! I still suspect foul play.

It then brightened up no end and whilst the golf had been spoiled, we could look forward to a nice warm night out on the beer.

Along with Jon and a first timer Robbo, who became an extremely popular regular, I went off to get some food. We had a McDonalds actually. By the time we caught up with the lads in a bar, a few of them were already well on their way. Most notably Alan, who was wearing a gaudy blue and yellow stripy shirt that assisted in the identification of him to anyone who might be interested. That's relevant here; trust me.

And then Eddie started to scream.

Eddie is yet to be introduced to you dear reader. He retired from the force in 2012 after over thirty-three years' service as a front line PC. He is a force legend. And as soon as he had left, he went straight back as a jailer in the busiest custody suite in the force area. Leeds was Eddie's first trip.

He is quite possibly the most well-known member of the force there has ever been. He is a unique character.

Prior to the second annual Norfolk Street Open, a golf competition I organised in 1998, Eddie had approached me and asked if he could attend. I knew him a little bit by then and like everyone else I already liked him a lot. It is impossible not to.

Eddie asked me if he could come to the tournament and when I responded that I didn't know he played, he said he didn't, he intended to start but, in the meantime, could he come and caddy for me?

I agreed and was then immediately bombarded with questions about attire, etiquette and the rules. I made sure to tell him to leave his jeans at home and to ensure his shirt had a collar of some sort.

As I said, I had started this tournament the year before. In 1997 I had come in plumb last with some crappy points total, so was hardly in a position to be advising a caddy on the way forward. I told him I wasn't very good and suggested he caddy for PD or Maurice. He declined.

He said he was caddying for me and that was final.

I drove into the car park on the appointed day to find Eddie setting up some kind of ribbon between two posts on the first tee. He was wearing a pair of black police trousers, a crew neck white tee shirt but with a tie and braces and a bowler hat. I parked up and went over for a closer look.

Printed on the front of his shirt was '*Simon Shuttleworth's Bag Man*' On the back it said, '*Norfolk Street's No.1 Golfer*'.

He proceeded to address the gathered thirty odd players in order to announce that after a temporary blip in 1997 I was here to win and they would all know about it every time I hit a good shot as the bugle would sound.

He then produced a pukka brass bugle and sounded the charge as though he was a bit part actor in a John Wayne US Cavalry film. He could actually play the thing properly. Well, he could if you want to hear a Cavalry charge or *Once in Royal David's City*. Come to think of it he plays the latter on his harmonica not his bugle but I digress.

Next, he invited me up to cut the ribbon and announce the 1998 Norfolk Street Open officially underway. I wasn't first off, so I had the time to plead with him not to do anything too illegal in golfing terms as we watched the first couple of groups get underway.

Soon it was my turn and spurred on by loud words of encouragement and as I recall, a shoulder massage, I knocked one away with my three wood. It was fair to crap down the right-hand side of the long par four opener and into the light-ish rough which was at that time full of brand new staked trees from which you could take a drop without penalty.

I duly dropped my ball onto a playable spot and spanked a seven iron over the water and up to the foot of the green. Tiger Woods would have wept but for me it was rather good.

Then I nearly shat myself as Eddie, standing two feet behind me, let go with the bugle followed by a massive yell. Maurice, who at the time was on the committee at the club we were at, buried his face in his hands.

I've been friends with Eddie ever since. He was Santa at my kids' primary school Christmas Fair for many years. They and my wife, Katy, think he is fantastic. Whenever he sees Katy, he drops to one knee and kisses her hand.

Anyway, back to Leeds in 2000 and Eddie screaming in a bar. It wasn't a scream of alarm or even a scream at anyone in particular. It was more like an impression of an air raid siren.

A lot of people looked round and over stomped a bouncer to tell us all as a group that if Eddie persisted, we would all be chucked out. Alan and his stripy shirt got a stern look for some sarcastic observation.

Eddie screamed again and that was it. Same miserable bouncer *'You've been warned, now get t'fuck out.'*

I had only had one more pint by this time so was comparably one of the more sober people present. I stood outside waiting for the lads to wander out and as I did so I spoke to a friendlier looking doorman. I put forward the view that we had not really done anything worthy of an ejection and he confessed in a low voice that it was down to the boss who had discovered we were cops and was not a fan.

The man I was talking to confided that he had nothing against us and I was right, we had done nothing wrong. He had, he said, got an application with the West Yorkshire Police pending.

Then the head honcho walked up. The same guy who had kicked us out. He was a six foot six giant. As he reached us, I was standing, hands in pockets speaking to the first man.

'Look at us mate. We are hardly being confrontational, are we?', I said.

The new arrival, in full Geoffrey Boycott vernacular, chipped in:

'Tha'd better go and tell that to tha friend wi' t' stripy shirt on. I just asked him to leave and he told me I'd better go and get some of me fuckin mates then'

I asked for and got permission to go back in and using the 1987 police training college 'push to chest' for probably the only ever time, I propelled Alan out and up the street, pausing only for him to tell the big doorman that he *'dressed like shit'.*

After a few more beers we decided to try the Majestic Nightclub. This was the place that a couple of years later was to make national headlines and to be of particular interest to Leeds United supporters like me when the Lee Bowyer / Jonathan Woodgate incident flared up there.

On the way in I was with Jason, Alan and a CID veteran famous for his short arms and deep pockets called Boris. The door staff stopped us immediately and pointed at Alan.

One of them said, *'he's not coming in, he's arseholed.'*

Mercifully, Alan didn't open his mouth and Jason was able to appeal to whatever slice of better nature there was available. He promised faithfully to take personal responsibility for Alan and ensure he didn't do anything daft.

You know as well as I do that bouncers are like refs. You can argue all you like but they will never change their minds. This was the exception. Jase was warned that they would take him to his word and hold him personally responsible for Alan's behaviour in the club.

What could possibly go wrong?

We had been in there for two minutes when we realised we had lost him. The three of us did a walking search of all the bars, dance floors and toilets. Nothing. We met by the main bar and considered what to do. We ordered a drink and after a couple more I suppose we, well sort of forgot about him.

Just then, Eddie called me over. *'Shutts, you've got a cat haven't you?'* he asked.

In the list of top 500 questions you get asked in a nightclub, this one doesn't appear.

'Yes' I replied, suspiciously.

Having established that my cat was called Tigger, he pointed to two blokes standing by the bar no more than a yard away. Both were vaguely familiar to me but I couldn't put names to either of them.

Eddie told me that they were both in Emmerdale, the TV programme. Until that moment I hadn't realised it wasn't still called Emmerdale Farm. I don't watch soaps and I last saw this particular one when Amos Brearley was running the Woolpack pub in it in the 1970s and my Mum watched every episode.

When Eddie revealed that the two 'actors' he had spotted played vets in Emmerdale, I knew where we were going with the cat questions.

I was too late to stop him as he asked them if they could have a look at my cat, Tigger. They were polite at first but ultimately Eddie was always going to be told to sod off. And he was. I'm guessing they'd heard it before. Eddie said they had hurt his feelings. He is a sensitive chap.

We had a decent night and several beers before finally deciding we would knock it on the head. We walked out through the main entrance but as we did Jason was grabbed by a large bouncer whose background as an intellectual conversationalist was not extensive.

'Oi, come here tha fuckin twat!'

Jason looked worried and enquired in a best disguised Lancashire accent as to what, perchance, the problem may be.

'I'll tell thee what t' fuckin problem is you twat. The problem, is the fuckin dick head tha said tha would vouch for on t' way in.'

We all remembered Alan at the same time. *'Oh yeah' said Jason, 'what happened to him, we lost him..?'*

The bouncer considered whether to believe Jason or not. He must have decided to do so.

'We had to kick the idiot out after about one minute' he said.

We left.

We ended up in different taxis but having got back to The Albatross I found myself locked out of the back yard with Boris, Eddie and Lee, another trip regular over the years. There was an obvious option to climb over quite a high wall to get in.

Boris and Eddie were a combination of too pissed and too old to attempt it. Lee was just too pissed but did manage to give me a leg up and over I went, ripping my shirt at the same time.

The next morning at breakfast, in walked Alan, looking none too comfortable.

'My ribs' he complained. *'I think I've had a kickin' or something. My ribs are killing me'.*

Brighton 2001.

WE WENT to Brighton during the 2001 General Election. I might have voted at that time for a Conservative Party who needed all the votes they could get. As it was, probably as part of a fiendish plan by Tony Blair, the election was planned so that I could not vote. Well, I suppose I could have done it by post but to be quite honest I really didn't care and he was always going to win. In those days, a good proportion of police officers voted Tory. This all changed for many when the Home Secretary and PM to be, Mrs May, alienated thousands at the stroke of a pen.

Anyway, Brighton was something of a paradox. It was one of the best and one of the worst in terms of enjoyment. The course was up to then and probably on balance remains my favourite. We played at the East Brighton Golf Club, near to the famous Roedean Girls School and it was magnificent. The hotel though, whilst clean and tidy, was one of my worst picks.

We were a bit limited for choice that we could afford as Brighton tends to be somewhat more expensive than your average town. I booked us into a small hotel that unfortunately didn't have a bar. It meant that the nights out were a bit disjointed as people wandered off in small groups looking for a pint and I didn't see some people at all away from the course.

On the first night there, we went out looking for a bar with the football on. England were playing Greece, hardly a footballing powerhouse nation, in a World Cup Qualifier. We found a Yates's bar with it on and joined the crowds.

I was with a few people including Scouse, a laid-back off the course but foul tempered on the course, career detective, who came on a few trips. He is a red through and through and a Hillsborough survivor. I am a lifelong Leeds United supporter and over the years we have had the odd friendly football debate. The 2020 lockdown year was at least a good one for the two of us in football terms as Liverpool ended their long wait to win the Premier League and Leeds joined them there by winning the Championship.

In the televised game, England progressed at a moderate pace and were totally underwhelming in their quest to overhaul quite poor opponents. I think we were actually winning 1-0 but were looking in danger of conceding and unlikely to score again when I decided to impart my thoughts to Scouse, who was standing just in front of me, a little nearer the large screen TV, which was high up on the wall.

'Your useless mate Fowler needs to get off if we are going to get a goal' I ventured.

That got a look. It was blasphemy of course to a man who believed the little chubby, touchline sniffing striker was in fact the almighty, God himself. *'He is shit tonight son. We need Smithy on to get amongst them.'*

I referred to Alan Smith, the exciting young Leeds United Striker who had burst onto the scene a couple of years before with a winning goal for us at Anfield. Smithy liked to make his presence felt and picked up the occasional card for his trouble.

Scouse turned away from the boring football, to take issue with my blasphemy. I was now watching it over his shoulder as he faced me. There was movement on the England bench, one of the officials had the subs board in hand.

'Alan Smith is a useless twat' said Scouse. I could see now that the fourth official was holding aloft the board with a nine on it. God's number was up.

'He is not fit to shine Robbie's boots,' continued the wise one as I watched Fowler turn and start to come off.

'I bet you ten quid here and now he will never play for England. He is just not good enough. Ten quid' he said, holding out his hand as I looked at Smithy, togged up, jumping on the spot as he waited for Fowler to run towards him.

I reached forward to take the offer of the guaranteed tenner but just as I did, my poker face must have betrayed me and Scouse turned round, snatching his hand away as Smith ran on for his first cap. He didn't score but he tried harder than Fowler, made the difference, someone else did net and England won 2-0. Of course, the funny thing is that Greece, in fact, went on to win the European Championships in 2004 while England's fifty plus years of hurt go on. And on.

A bit later some of us fetched up in a bar next to the pebble beach in a place I think is called 'The Arches'. Eddie was there and I went over to speak to him. I can't remember who it was but someone asked him if he was going for a dip in the sea. Eddie is well-known for going for a swim in his pants when the mood takes. That is usually if it is sunny and we are playing cricket on the beach. Eddie said that he wouldn't be, not at night, not in the rain.

We had been told that a storm was coming through the south coast and was likely to rip across the course as we were playing it on Thursday morning. As we looked out of the open door of the bar, the storm came early. Torrential rain lashed down and the wind howled.

The waves reared up and crashed into the edge of the pebbles. Nature at its best – it was great to watch. Then the idiot who was daring Eddie to go in the sea suggested that he was losing his bottle in his old age.

Eddie has never bottled anything in his life.

In ten seconds flat his clothes were on the floor in the bar and he was striding – in his Y-fronts – across the pebbles. He went up and over a ridge and down towards the roaring ocean. Phil, the Skegness para roll merchant and I followed with one or two others, all getting drenched in the rain and sea spray.

As we looked down at Eddie, we could see he had walked straight into the surf and he turned to face us inthigh deep water. He was yelling something but the roar of the waves was deafening and I couldn't tell what he was saying.

We edged a bit closer but as we did so a huge wave took his legs from under him and he went down. When the wave had receded, Eddie had gone. Visibility was terrible and the rain was coming even harder. I think my heart actually stopped beating for a second.

I looked at Phil. For a moment neither of us knew what to do – there was no one to rescue, just continuous enormous waves. I saw myself going straight back to Leicester to see Eddie's better half, Trish.

'It's like this Trish; we've lost Eddie....' I was saying. This would be the fourth and last ever Central Golf Trip.

We moved forward to see if we could get a better look and as we did this the twat suddenly appeared ten yards to the right but no further out. He raised both arms as though he had just scored the winner at Wembley and roared a victory roar.

Back in the bar he was first applauded home and then bought various large measures of spirits by all and sundry. If he fell off the roof of John Lewis, Eddie would land the right way up in a new suit. Or as my Dad used to say, if he fell in a pile of shit, he would come up smellin' of roses.

As for the golf, well the early storm had done us a favour and the sun shone. The course was magnificent. It was a real test of anyone's game but to me it was just beautifully laid out with great views and spectacular holes.

To cap it all I won something. I managed to win the King Rabbit prize for the best twenty-four plus handicapper. My only solo victory in all of the trips.

The next night was fairly uneventful save for some fun in a nightclub. Two of our number, not regulars and I'll spare their blushes by not naming them, decided to strip off and dance bollock naked on the main dance floor. The standard of this place was perhaps best summed up by the fact that two, presumably local blokes, were spotted standing at the bar drinking their own piss.

Anyway, one of our two tackle out twisters decided it was time to visit the loo. He got dressed and went to use one of the cubicles but had to wait a minute before two extremely suspicious individuals came out together, one of them wiping his nose.

On his way out I bumped into him in the corridor and asked him how he was. He had to shout his reply because the music was very loud.

'Strange fucking place Shutts!' he yelled.

Before I could reply a passing bouncer interrupted: *'Oi, watch your language or you'll be out.'*

'Watch my language?' said our man. *'Watch my fucking language? I am slaughtered and I've just been dancing out there with my cock out. Then I see two blokes drinking piss at the bar while your bar staff are plonking lagers down all around them. Then I need a shit and I have to wait for the local coke merchant to finish a deal before I can get in a cubicle. And you're telling me to mind my fucking language. Are you taking the piss?'*

The bouncer just shrugged, said, *'OK fair enough'* and walked off.

A group of us tried to decide where the best place would be for late night card school. In the end we bought a load of booze and went back to the lounge at the B&B.

There was a night watchman on duty for part of the night, a nice old chap in his late seventies called Harry, who couldn't do enough for us. He got us glasses for our beer and made sure we were all ok. He said he would be turning in about 3am but we were welcome to stay in the lounge.

We were all polite to him except Blackie, another CID man who left Leicester the following year for the sunnier climes of Devon. He stayed as a regular golf tripper though. He is a quality golfer and a man who could probably give me lessons in dry sarcasm. Those who know me but don't know him would tell you that is some feat indeed.

To be fair he *is* very funny and up there with PD as possibly the best natural golfer to ever come on the trips. In the B&B though, he spent his time taking the piss out of Harry. Just little comments about age and infirmity that Harry apparently either ignored or didn't hear.

It got to 3am and the card game was still going on when Harry stuck his head round the door and said, *'Right then lads, I'm off to bed. Don't get too noisy and please don't leave a mess or the boss will have the arse with me.'*

Blackie looked up and said '*I bet you'll only have to get up for a couple of pisses, going to bed this late won't you Harry? I imagine it's normally half a dozen a night at your age.*'

Harry seemed to sigh and then he stepped fully inside the room. It was a Blackie comment too many.

'*You lads are a good bunch,*' he said '*Top lads. Nice manners and well-behaved – better than some we get in here.*'

Then he turned and pushed his glasses down his nose, looking over the top of them at Blackie and said, '*Apart from you son. You're a fucking twat.*'

Aberystwyth 2002

SOMETIMES I would ask Alan or Jason what they thought about a location before I booked it. On the odd occasion though I was either too busy at work or just couldn't be bothered, so I just sorted something out.

And so it was in 2002, having spent a year back in uniform I came into the CID for my first substantive posting as a Detective Sergeant at Asfordby Street, still within the Central Area, and the busiest posting in terms of serious crime involving firearms, drugs and robbery.

One lunchtime I was thinking about the trip when I noticed, in a golf guide someone had left lying around, that the course in Aberystwyth was well recommended. On the spur of the moment, I selfishly sorted a week out when I was already due to be off on the Thursday and Friday so I wouldn't use much leave up. I then phoned the course, booked the golf and found a hotel on the sea front, near to the course, that did us a decent deal.

I had no idea what Aberystwyth was like.

When I sent the email out announcing the trip the most common response was *'Where?'* The only enthusiasm came from Ben, who was only too happy to be returning to his university town.

On the day, a decent sized group of us were on site and checked in just after lunchtime. Eddie was paying suspicious attention to a nice conference room at the hotel, with an expensive looking glass topped meeting table. I saw him talking to one of the staff and I asked his mate Barney what he was up to.

Barney replied, '*No idea but he has got something that absolutely reeks. All the way down here the car has stunk like rotting food. I had my head out the window most of the time.*'

I forgot about it for a while as we went and had a few beers and then decided to have a game of barefoot footy on the beach. This is difficult on Aberystwyth beach as the sand is deep and full of stones which is not ideal if you are barefoot. We got fed up with this quite soon and decided to settle it with a penalty shoot-out which my team won four or five nil by the simple exponent of putting Ben in goal. Well, there is no sense losing when you have someone on your team who was a trainee keeper at Middlesbrough FC.

Later, once the stragglers had turned up and we all met up in the hotel for a drink, Eddie started to gather us together for what he said was a special treat. The thing with these bookings was that usually the hotel would take my credit card details and I would be personally responsible for any damages. The thought of an Eddie-inspired treat made me fear for my bank balance.

Anyway, he told us he had booked the conference room with the glass topped table and he marshalled us all inside and then said he'd be two minutes. The room was about thirty feet long and initially we milled around the room wondering where he had gone to.

His reappearance pushed us all down to one end away from him. He was carrying a bag of something that was absolutely rank. It stunk the place out. From the bag he produced a chicken. He apologised, telling us that he had bought it earlier than he should have and, in all probability, he should have frozen it. Now it was past its sell by date.

He looked at Barney. Barney called him a knob.

Eddie put the chicken on the table and announced that there was to be a competition between Blackie and Alan, as they were about to leave Leicestershire for Devon and Cornwall Constabulary. In the event, Alan changed his mind but at the time they were both set to leave.

The competition, set to music, involved the two of them having one minute each to see who could stuff the most golf balls up the chicken. I have no idea who won. Most of us were concentrating on holding our noses and mouth breathing.

There were then a few more antics, one of which involved Scouse and a lad called Davo eating raw leeks. I'm sure I put it to Scouse not all that long ago that he threw up in a carrier bag after this game but he denied it. Maybe he didn't, I can't remember.

What I do remember is Davo in the pub just afterwards. His breath was so bad it was ridiculous. The leek is of course a member of the onion family. We spent the first half hour there getting him to stand two metres away from the rest of us while we ordered him different drinks to see if one might help with the smell. You could say we were the original pioneers of social distancing. Half a bottle of Grand Marnier does not work, just in case you find yourself in the same situation.

Eddie we love you but you really are stark raving mad, as Barney discovered the next morning when he couldn't get out of bed because Eddie had placed his wardrobe, open door facing down, over the top of him as he lay there.

Anyway, we had a better than expected night out. There was only one club in the town and this was on the sea front next to a karaoke bar on a kind of pier. A few of us enrolled for the karaoke and one or two got to perform. Our ex-Marine, Jon, was one. He can't sing but he was enthusiastic.

We listened to a few others, some of which were OK and then suddenly Blackie was up there. Now, Blackie will usually have a plan and this was no exception. He's not a singer so he had worked out that he needed the crowd to do the hard yards. He picked '*Delilah*' and all he had to do was lead the masses to the water. Everyone was full of beer and everyone knew the words. It worked a treat.

When it was time to announce the results, the compere handed out the third placed prize to someone who could actually sing and then he announced that in second place, for giving a rousing rendition of *Tom Jones's Delilah*......it was Blackie.

Blackie wasn't listening at this point so Jon, quick as a flash jumped up and accepted the prize from the compere who looked a bit confused but handed it over. When Jon then went back pretending to be the winner the bloke was just in the process of giving him that one as well when he realised what was going on and told Jon to sod off.

We ended up in the club which was OK and one of our brethren was seen sneaking off up the road with an attractive young lady. The next morning at breakfast, the boys obviously wanted some sordid details. He was a single lad but he's not now, so I'll spare his blushes and call him Joe.

'Did you get your leg over then son?' was one of the cleaner versions of the question.

'No,' he said, *'She was dead keen and she wants to see me again tonight but I didn't have a condom last night so I only got a blow job.'*

Anyway, we went off for the golf and in the *Texas Scramble* round we really were impressed with this quality golf course. It stayed mainly dry, which helped, but big dark clouds were approaching and it was clear that a wet afternoon in the main *Stableford* competition was on the cards.

As I came off the course for lunch I suddenly needed the facilities quite urgently. A combination of a good few beers and a kebab with a full English in the morning and nature was taking its course. Unfortunately, when I got to the gents I discovered two cubicles occupied and the other one flooded.

I found the steward, who I had got to know in my capacity as the trip organiser. He took pity on my plight.

He said, *'Here's the key to the lady members' locker room. None of them are in and I doubt they will be as its about to chuck it down.'*

Well, it was lovely in there. For a start it was carpeted and everywhere was spotless. There was even a Woman's Weekly on a coffee table, so I took that in with me to read the problem pages. Bliss.

By God though did I unload. For a moment it was even slightly distressing. I thought I was going to empty and they'd find me hanging on the back of the door; a costume of a man as Mickey Flanagan once said.

I got through it though and apart from the fact that my own stink was making me slightly nauseous, it was quite a nice feeling. I was hungry and ready for some lunch.

It turned out that the steward was wrong though. Just as I was about to leave the locker room, two lady members came in. There was an awkward moment where they looked at me and I looked at them.

Then I handed one of them the key and said, *'I'd give that ten minutes if I were you.'*

All predictions about the afternoon were correct. It absolutely threw it down. As a result, the golf was less than memorable. About the only thing of note was that a couple of teddies got chucked out of their prams. One was Scouse's who quit halfway round because he was playing badly and he hated playing in the rain. I'm 100% with him on both of those. Unfortunately, as the organiser I had to grin and bear it.

The other one was a proper baby sulk from a profoundly serious golfer called Trevor who had been on the previous two trips to Leeds and Brighton and won both times. He was playing off thirteen at the time although he was often better than that. This year he was having a nightmare in the rain, playing with Brett and Craig, two of the nicest guys you could meet and both eighteen handicappers, so they knew their way round a course.

Trevor decided (he told others this, not me to my face), that I had deliberately placed him with 'two *crap* players' to lessen his chances of winning and to increase the chances of people I liked more.

Utter rubbish. I never did give a toss who won, apart from near the end of the trips, when I would have liked Alan to win as he is a good player and he was, apart from me, the only ever present on them all. Spoiler alert: He never won. He cocked it up every time.

Anyway, this year, erstwhile Middlesbrough FC trainee Ben won handsomely off a sixteen handicap. Or a crap standard as Trevor would have said. Keep smiling, it's only a game.

After the golf we sorted ourselves out for good night out and eventually we ended up in the same nightclub near to the sea front. This was after a decent meal in a restaurant owned by an uncle of Eddie's roommate, Barney.

I remember having a good time in the club, right up until one of the bouncers came up and said it was probably best if we took our drunk mate out now. It was kicking out time, more or less and I was pleased to see it wasn't Alan this time but Kev, someone a whole lot less aggressive when he's drunk.

Kev was a softly spoken lad and another one who moved on to a different force in the south. On this occasion he was totally shit-faced. I got hold of Jason who was rooming with him and we took an arm each. The bouncers couldn't have been more different from the stereotypical view of their profession – accurate as that has been for me many times. They were laughing and wishing us well with him as we took an arm each and turned him round, football ejection style, to walk him out backwards.

He didn't resist and we were able to get him in to the fresh air and let him go just before he *let go*, all over the nice clean streets of Aberystwyth. Once he'd got that out of his system, he seemed a bit better and the three of us started walking back to the hotel.

As we set off, we were joined by Jon and Robbo. Jon immediately noticed Joe walking in the opposite direction with the same young lady he had left with on the previous night.

'Oi Joe!' yelled Jon at the top of his voice. *'Another blow job is it?!'*

Most of the street stopped and turned at that one. Including the young lady, who's head shot round like it was on a swivel.

We carried on and back at the hotel we found them willing to serve us booze, so someone went to get some cards. I don't always play but sometimes stick around for a drink and to enjoy the banter. After about five minutes, in walked Joe.

'Shit, sorry mate,' said a sheepish Jon. *'Did I drop you in it?'*

'No,' said Joe, *'She did say "how do they know that?" and I just said, well, I told them.'*

'So she binned you?' I asked.

'Oh no, she still wanted me to stay but I said, you know what, I think I'd rather play cards.'

The next morning, a few sore heads set off on the informal eighteen or whatever people could manage on the last day. Jason and Kev were supposed to be in a four ball with me and another player but Jase turned up on his own.

'Where's Vomiting Victor?' I asked. *'I hope he's not still in bed. It's a 10am check out.'*

'No' said Jason. *'He's in the back of my car, the twat. He threw up all over the room and there's fuck all to clean it up with. I ended up getting most of it up with a spoon'*

Between the ninth and tenth holes at Aberystwyth, you have to walk through the car park. As we passed Jason's car, we banged on the window to wake *Sleeping Beauty* up to remind him what a good mate Jase was.

Back in the CID I got involved in an investigation into a robbery at an Alliance and Leicester Building Society. The robbery was on Uppingham Road in Leicester and at the time I was the DS at Asfordby Street. We neighboured the policing area which actually covered the building society.

On this particular day in August, three characters decided to withdraw some money without a bank card. Two went inside and jumped up onto and over the counter – this was before the days of full screens. The third man was the lookout outside. The robbers terrified the staff and had it away with a few thousand pounds. The staff were threatened with weapons but none were actually seen.

The OIC was a young DC from the local station called Chris. He was a hardworking and productive lad who had a good career. I was tasked to assist and supervise his investigation and I took along one of my DCs, now a good friend and a onetime golf tripper called Tim. Tim is extraordinarily laid back. He speaks slowly and never sounds stressed. He is 6'4" tall and extremely calm and capable in tense situations, without ever seeming threatening.

By the end of the month, we had identified both of the two counter jumpers; one had been arrested and charged, the other was living in Peckham; we didn't know where but we knew when he was due to sign on for his dole cheque. The lookout's identity was still not known.

So, Tim and I, plus Chris and another officer who was, shall we say, not the most robust individual, organised an overnighter. This meant we would be able to have a beer, stay in a hotel, then get up and go to make the arrest. This was to take place at a job centre in Camberwell. Tim was put in charge of accommodation.

Nowadays, cops doing overnighters get the hotel booked for them by an agency and can claim evening meal expenses on top. It costs forces a small fortune. Back then it was a straight £47 fee or £57 if you were in London. How you spent it was up to you. You could sleep in a ditch if you liked and spend all the money in the pub. Tim booked us into a cheap hotel in Blackheath and we shared rooms. That left us enough to afford several beers and a curry. The only downside was his snoring but hey, at least *he* got a good night's sleep.

At breakfast I went through the plan. Chris and I would go into the job centre and stand behind the counter with the staff. Tim and the other DC would stay by the front doors. When chummy signed on, Chris and I would follow him out having called Tim to tell him we were on our way. Tim or the other DC would make the arrest as the guy left the building and all four of us would be there just in case things turned ugly. We all wore stab vests and we carried retractable batons and rigid cuffs in covert holsters. A marked Met Police van would then emerge from a hiding place around the back and we'd whisk him away.

Then the problems started. We had spent the evening taking the piss out of the other DC because he told us he was going to drink us under the table. We ended up finishing his beer. Tim doesn't get drunk under many tables but this lad was not even a contender.

Now our lightweight colleague caused further difficulties: '*Right, as soon as he comes out I'm going to take him out, baton across the backs of his legs.*'

I said, '*No, you're not. You're going to do what I have just said you will do. No weapons were seen on this job and the risk assessment hasn't highlighted any. If he cuts up, we will deal with it. He's only a little bloke anyway. Tim stop grinning.*'

The DC wouldn't have it though. He was clearly extremely nervous. I couldn't rely on him so I switched the roles. I would be outside with Tim. He would be inside with Chris, something Chris was less than enamoured with.

At the job centre we took up our positions. I stood on the pavement by the front door, able to step into the path of anyone coming out and turning left. Tim took the other side. As we waited there, trying to look inconspicuous, a car pulled up on the opposite side of the street. Out got the driver carrying a blue A4 hardback book. This is the number one national identifier of a CID officer.

He obviously didn't know we had a job on, or he wouldn't have parked there. There was nothing we could do. I studied my shoes and at first I didn't see a little drunk man come up to me. I soon smelled him though. Booze, B.O., halitosis and piss, all rolled into one.

'Watch out son. It's the filth' he said.

'What?' I said, realising he was talking to me.

'It's the fucking bill mate. Pigs. That lad over there with that blue book.'

'Are you sure?'

'Oh yeah. I can fucking smell 'em mate. Not much gets past me.'

Not many cans of White Lightning get past you, I was thinking, but I thanked him for the tip and he shuffled off, his foul smell following on after about five minutes.

Before long Tim and I saw who we thought was our guy going in. Sure enough my mobile trilled and it was Chris confirming he was signing on and then giving us the off as he turned for the door.

In the event he turned right out the front door and all five foot seven of him walked straight into Tim's chest. Tim took hold of him and told him he was under arrest on suspicion of robbery at the Alliance and Leicester Building Society on Uppingham Road in Leicester on the relevant date.

He said, *'Fuck off man, I've never even been to Leicester'*

Tim said, *'Yeah you have mate. You jumped over the counter, didn't you?'*

'Oh, was that Leicester?' he said. *'I thought we were in Coventry when we did that one.'*

We took him back to Leicester via Camberwell Police Station and he was a laugh. He told Tim and I that he had never been dealt with by cops like us. We spent the entire journey taking the piss. I think he was used to a sterner approach but that wasn't our style.

The next day my Dad was having a heart bypass operation and by coincidence Tim had a similar family emergency so neither of us went in to interview him about the offence. He was dealt with by our nervous DC friend and another officer.

They must have done a decent job because he not only put his hands up fully, he also gave them the name of the lookout, who had been hard to identify because there was only a poor quality external CCTV picture of him. Unlike the other two, he never went inside the building.

A team of four, without me or Tim, hotfooted it back to London to make the third and final arrest. They picked the man up just where our little friend had said he would be. They decided to interview him at Camberwell Police Station instead of bringing him back to Leicester.

When they asked him where he was on the relevant day, he gave an unusual answer.

'*At school*', he said. '*I'm a maths teacher. If you speak to the headteacher, he will confirm I was teaching year nines' that day, all day.*'

They did. He was. He had never set foot in a police station before. Or an Alliance and Leicester Building Society.

The lad we had arrested at the job centre had been charged but he had to come back to the police station for some more questioning about other offences. Tim and I were back and we had a word with him. We asked him why he had given our colleagues the name of an innocent maths teacher as the third suspect.

He said, '*Oh, I was at school with him. I never liked him and when you two left me with your mate dealing with me, I thought I'd have a bit of fun.*' Our lightweight nervous colleague was winning friends everywhere. We laughed like drains. The diminutive robber should really have been charged with wasting police time but it was too funny. The CPS don't need any encouragement *not* to charge people so with a lack of enthusiasm from us he walked on that one.

It's worth noting that Chris carried on and got a commendation for the job, potting the two main offenders, including our comical friend and watching them get locked up for lengthy spells.

Bath 2003

IN JANUARY 2003, while still a DS in the CID at Asfordby Street I picked up probably one of the more unusual and most gruesome jobs of my career. I had gone over to the area base at Charles Street to see my DI when the call came in that uniformed officers were responding to a possible suspicious death on a residential street off the main A47 road which leads out of Leicester and carries on all the way to the Norfolk coast.

A man called Peter Andrews had called his social worker to tell her that he needed to see her. He was a diagnosed paranoid schizophrenic man who was, bizarrely, the carer for his own mother, also schizophrenic. His social worker told him that she couldn't drop everything to come over but she did remind him that she was due to see him the next day to give him his fortnightly injection.

Andrews insisted. He told her she must attend immediately because his mum was dead. He said he had killed her by chopping off her head with a chainsaw. The social worker, a highly competent and hardworking professional, was initially stunned into action and was halfway out of the door when her boss stopped her and asked her what she was doing. Suitably appraised he told her to call the police first and then go, with their protection.

The first officers on scene were an experienced officer called Adam with an officer of six weeks' operational experience under Adam's supervision; a *sprog,* as we used to call them in the days when they put the kettle on without asking why they should have to.

Adam and his sprog arrived at exactly the same time as the social worker and found Andrews sitting on the back doorstep in the back yard of the house he shared with his mum.

He looked up as they arrived and took in the presence of the cops. '*I wondered why it took you so long*', he said.

The officers allowed the social worker to walk into the house ahead of them. Suddenly she cried out.

'*Oh my God, he has as well!*'

Adam looked past her into the hall and could see the decapitated head of a female lying on the floor near to a doorway, staring back at him. He walked past the head and saw a chainsaw plugged in at a socket in what looked like the lounge. Adam went on to become a particularly good self-defence trainer and the instincts for this future job were obviously present then. He quickly realised two things. One: this man has followed me into the house. Two: that bloody chainsaw is live. In one motion he pulled the plug on the chainsaw then whipped round and shoving Andrews against a wall, quickly handcuffed him to the rear.

On the way to the police station Andrews did not shut up. He told Adam that he had sliced through his mum's neck with a chainsaw and that it was like a knife through butter. He said he had practiced with various brands on joints of meat in the garden before settling on a Bosch saw he found in the Littlewoods catalogue. He said the Germans had won World War Three and now controlled the planet using satellites on Mars. He said no one could hurt her now and no one could take her from him.

It didn't look like it was going to be one of the harder cases to prove but it still had a few surprises in store for us. The first came when the scene was examined. The body of Joan Andrews was lying chest down on the sofa in the lounge. Her head was a few feet away in the doorway to the hall. There should have been blood everywhere but there was not. Just a huge puddle of it under the sofa.

The pathologist was of the view that at the point that Joan was decapitated, she was either dead or at the point of death. The interviews would be interesting, always assuming Andrews was going to be passed as fit for interview. In the end, after making another torrent of admissions to the police medical examiner, a psychiatrist said that he could be interviewed provided he had an appropriate adult and the interviews were short and to the point.

The interviews were led by a good mate of mine called Fergy, assisted by his crew mate from the recently formed Leicestershire Major Crime Team. They were supplied to us just for the interview process. Fergy was a very conscientious detective and an excellent interviewer.

Andrews made the same admissions about the chainsaw and added plenty more about Germans and satellites. He cleared up the pathology when he told Fergy that he had mixed up twenty of his mum's tablets into her evening drink and waited until she had finished it and fallen asleep on the sofa before he carried out his awful act.

One enquiry led a detective called Frankie to the nearest butcher's shop, only a five minute walk from the scene. By the time of his visit, the crime, awful that it was, was the talk of the area. Frankie quickly established that Andrews, known in the shop by description, had been in to buy meat several times in the preceding weeks. The proprietor explained what he had wanted.

'*He initially asked me if he could have a side of beef*' said the butcher, '*but I explained that since the BSE crisis we don't sell them anymore*'

'*OK*' said Frankie. '*So, did he buy anything else from you*?'

'*Oh yes*' said the butcher. '*He asked me what the biggest joint I had was and I told him it was a leg of lamb so he bought one. Then he was back the next week for another and then another. God knows what he was doin...oh God, oh no.....*'

Frankie had to get the butcher a chair.

Now, when I think back to times like these, I can see that we operated on a different plane to the majority of normal law abiding people. That butcher was genuinely distressed just by his comparatively small part in the investigation. To us, it was gruesome and it was far from normal but it was what we did and we just got on with it.

My small team from Asfordby Street took on the bulk of the tasks, preparing for court. The family of the victim were lovely people and they took to their excellent, caring Family Liaison Officer (FLO),

Danny. He discovered that Andrews had, a few months earlier, been made redundant from a job in a local factory.

It was, in truth, an act of kindness by the owner of the firm who had known the late Mr Andrews Senior. Peter was becoming dangerous around the machinery and many employers would have just got rid. This guy was honourable and let him go with some money in his pocket.

What Andrews did with it was slightly unusual. He rented a portacabin at a site near his home, had a full size snooker table installed and went there every day with his pack up and his radio and played snooker. It was something I mentioned to Fergy when I bumped into him a few weeks later, because he was actually an excellent snooker player himself, a hundred break man who had won a number of tournaments.

The next surprise came when I had Joan's blood tested for the medication that we thought must have killed her. The results didn't make sense. There was apparently no more than a therapeutic level of it in her system. Later with experience, I came to understand that this can be the case when a person has been on medication for a long time and their system is used to a particular drug.

The problem this created though was that we couldn't actually prove how Peter had killed Joan. He told us he had chopped her head off and we believed him but the pathologist was going to give us a report which said she was either dead or about to die when this happened. Peter had explained that by saying he had poisoned her but the toxicology did not support this assertion.

Our Crown Prosecution Service (CPS) lawyer was a woman called Elaine who is quite a direct person. We always got on really well. She has personality and whilst she can and will tear into cops of any standing she can take it when it comes back. Where we do beg to differ is on whose idea it was to charge Andrews with attempted murder. I know that it was mine. Elaine remembers it differently! Either way it was the simple way out. It was the offence we could actually prove against a man who was looking increasingly like he would be unfit to stand trial anyway.

This was borne out in court when the judge decreed that there would be no trial and Andrews was sentenced to a hospital order with restrictions meaning that he would only be freed if deemed fit by a Mental Health Tribunal. This did actually happen a few years later and the CPS, thanks to Elaine's efficiency, immediately ensured he went back to court where this time he did plead guilty to attempted murder and was sent straight back to custody.

Just prior to the CPS being told that Andrews was being considered for release, Fergy the original interviewer and by now a sergeant working elsewhere, had realised that his snooker game needed some remedial work. The national police championships were coming up and he had not been playing much so he entered a tournament in Leicester city centre.

When he arrived, he was told he was playing a guy he had to give a big handicap start to. Despite beginning at about sixty behind he managed to win the first frame because the other player was poor. Not only that, this individual hardly said a word and kept his head down, only ever conversing with another man who sat with him in between shots. Fergy thought he looked familiar but couldn't place where from.

You're ahead of me here aren't you?

Sure enough, after the next frame Fergy was told the match was conceded and before he had chance to ask why, he realised his opponent had left. When he was told that this was because the man was out on day release from an institution, the cogs began to fall into place and Fergy asked what the opponent's name was.....

Back in the world of golf I had decided to visit one of the country's more picturesque cities.

Bath was a good trip but I misjudged the distance to the golf club from the city centre hotel. The hotel itself was not bad quality and for social purposes it was great, right on the doorstep of all the pubs and clubs of this fantastic city.

The course though was within the grounds of Bath Racecourse and was miles away. Which meant a dodgy morning after drive for some people that they could have done without.

Colin was a guy who only came on a couple of trips. Nice lad, he was on traffic but despite that he was good company. On this trip though he did not endear himself to the group. He was the first of, thankfully, only a few to win with a forty plus points score. forty is the barrier that sets the hares racing. The C word is a touchy one but it does get used occasionally. What? No not that one. Wash your mouth out. This C word is *cheat!*

Yes, it is time to talk about *Banditry* in more detail.

I touched on it in Whitby, when PD was getting the arse with Maurice and it is fair to say he had the arse with a few other people over the years. PD is a proper golfer and it is generally the good players who get the most upset by banditry. This is understandable because they are naturally better than most of us and so they have the most to lose in a game.

So, what is banditry, I hear you ask.

Allow me to explain.

Golf is meant to be turned into an even battle by the handicap system. Each golf course has a *par*, which is a number, usually around seventy, meaning that a really good golfer should be able to play all eighteen holes of a course in seventy shots. Such a person would have a zero handicap, usually referred to as *scratch*.

However, then I come along and there is no way I can match that seventy shots. On average I might take ninety-eight shots to hit the ball around the same course. So, to give me a chance against this much better player we employ the handicap system. If my usual score is ninety-eight on that same course then my handicap would be twenty-eight. This means I get a twenty-eight shot allowance, sometimes reduced to three quarters of that in competitions, making my match against a scratch golfer a more even one.

Banditry is when you pretend that your handicap is higher than it really is to seek an advantage. Some people would say this is cheating but it is hard to pin down. This is because everyone can have a great day and you have to allow for that. I have always been a twenty-eight handicapper and I nearly always hit the ball around a par seventy course in something between ninety-seven and about 110. Very occasionally it might be slightly less or slightly more.

One day, playing Scouse and another mate off my twenty-eight handicap on a Par seventy course, I hit it around in ninety-one. This wasn't banditry because it was as rare as rocking horse shit and they knew it was just a good day at the office.

When Colin came to Bath in 2003 he played off nineteen. He was in reality more like a fifteen handicapper. He had a lovely swing and he could hit the ball a long way. If you play exactly to your handicap in a Stableford competition you usually score about thirty-six points. Colin got forty and that was after tailing off with a couple of dodgy holes near the end or it could have been forty-four.

The handicaps were always decided by me and Alan, usually in a meeting in the pub the night before. I had the casting vote. We really thought Colin was a nineteen. It was one of a few we got wrong over the years.

At the same time Blackie, one of two players with a single figure handicap was playing an absolute stormer. He hit the ball around the course in seventy-five shots, scoring thirty-eight points. He was by a country mile and then some, the best golfer there and he should have been the winner.

He was second to Colin and a lot of the boys were not happy. Blackie was virtually a permanent fixture on the trips after that and he never did win it. This was his big chance.

Colin though, is *not* a cheat, let me be clear. He is one of the good guys. He just misjudged handicap banter with a group including some people who didn't know him well and seeing his impressive style immediately thought he was a good player. Better than nineteen.

Anyway, the golf developed as I have described. Blackie was on fire in the morning *Texas Scramble* as well as his seventy-five in the afternoon *Stableford*. He led his team to a remarkable nine under par in the *Texas*. PD was on the warpath and when he realised that his own team's brilliant seven under had not won it, he stormed off chuntering under his breath about the CID.

PD played with Blackie in the afternoon though and he saw the seventy-five with his own eyes. To his credit he apologised and said he totally believed it now. Blackie was simply outstanding. Still, Colin's forty points soon gave PD someone else to focus on.

And then there was Mike. He is a mate of mine and Scouse's who only came to Bath as a caddy for Scouse. He doesn't play the game but liked the idea of a couple of nights away.

He lasted about thirty seconds.

Having seen several people hit the ball, as Bing Crosby sang, '*straight down the middle*', he then watched Scouse top his thirty yards into some bushes.

'Fuck that for a game of soldiers' he said. '*I'm not spending four hours carrying your bag watching that shit. I'm off.*'

And with that he dumped Scouse's bag, walked into the clubhouse and spent the day getting pissed and watching the racing on TV before he later got embroiled in some fun with a girl with a broken arm.

This was all during the evening once we were all scrubbed up and out in the city centre. Let's be generous and say she was nineteen or twenty. I was going to say I don't know where he found her but that's a little disingenuous because *she* very definitely found *him.*

And despite Mike's charming personality, Robert Redford-like chiselled jaw and Joe Wicks physique, she really fancied his mate. OK, Mike only has one of those attributes, but you get what I mean.

Mike was with Kev, the Aberystwyth Vomit King, when the young lady, who was quite attractive, spotted them. Kev was absolutely *not interested.* He was and I'm sure still is besotted with his then girlfriend and now wife. He was not the wandering type and he made this clear to Mike and Broken Arm Girl.

Where it got properly uncomfortable for Kev was when he was back in the room that he was sharing with Mike, on his own, trying to get to sleep. Mike walked in, followed by Broken Arm Girl. It looked like she had settled for her second choice but then she said, '*Your mate can join in if he wants.*'

This appealed to neither of the boys. Mike because, well, it just didn't and Kev because he was busy shitting himself wondering if his better half would believe that none of this was of his making. What I didn't know then was that Kev was not a paid up member of the '*What Goes on Tour*' club and that this was going to bite me and Scouse on the arse later in the week.

The next day, we had a chance little encounter with royalty during the friendly Friday round. I was playing in a group with Darren, who I had shared with in Leeds. He is a really quiet guy who is very proper and possibly the neatest, tidiest policeman I have ever met. He used to walk from the car park when he was a DC at Charles Street CID, about half a mile with his suit jacket on a hanger. I never knew why he didn't just put it on.

I wanted to play with Darren because two days later I was going to his wedding. It was going to be a full Hindu ceremony. Darren is a Cornishman but he was marrying a lovely Hindu girl called Row who is one of those people you just instantly like when you meet her.

Anyway, as we played, we were aware because they'd told us at the pro shop on the course, that Prince Charles was visiting Bath and his helicopter would be landing in the middle of the racecourse, which was right in the middle of the golf course.

I can't say I remembered seeing it land but I did see the convoy of three cars speeding along a road which bisected the fairway we were on. I saw the cars just after Darren played his shot towards them. Darren didn't see them until after he had played.

We watched helplessly as the ball skipped off the surface and smashed into the side of one of the cars. I don't know what we expected but all that happened was the Prince waved and smiled. It's only later when you think about it that you remember the cars would probably stop a 7.62 round, so he was hardly going to be concerned.

It was one for Darren's speech on Sunday anyway and it was a funny end to a decent trip.

My story of the week didn't end there though. On the Sunday Katy and I went to the wedding. It was a spectacular affair. Brilliant dress (I mean everyone not just the bride), great people and outstanding food. I got told off by one family member for trying to pass Darren a pint of lager during the ceremony. It was at a point where he had been in the same spot for about two hours and he looked parched. He did reach out for it but it was quickly snatched away.

While the ceremony was still going on, it was our turn to sit down to dinner, having got what we wanted from a buffet. I was with Katy and we sat with Scouse and his partner Lisa. On the opposite side of our table were Jason and Kev with their girlfriends.

I was just about to put my glass of beer to my lips when Jason's partner spoke to me.

'*That was a close run thing with Mike smuggling the girl into his room and Kev not wanting to join in, wasn't it Shutts?*' Kev's better half nodded her agreement.

Scouse spat his beer out.

Lisa just looked at him and Katy stared at me for what seemed like ages before speaking.

Then she said '*What the hell is this?! Women in the rooms? This is a new one. Why don't I know about this? What are YOU hiding?*'

'*My thoughts exactly*', said Lisa.

It turned out that Kev had carried on '*shitting himself*' metaphorically, about the events with Mike and Broken Arm Girl and had decided to get in first and tell his girlfriend what happened. Jason had backed him up.

Scouse and I had a quiet word with them afterwards.

WHAT GOES ON TOUR.......!

I have of course now realised the irony of that, coming from a man writing a book about it all.

Great Yarmouth 2004

IN 2004 'the Major' started to come on the trips. He is a career detective and long-time friend of several of the players, especially Blackie and Alan. His speeches are legendary. He has the knack of taking a set of real circumstances and exaggerating the facts beyond belief, turning it into a comedy.

Most of us have been the subject of one of his tales over the years. It was only really a problem for you if you let it get to you or worse, you tried to interrupt. He is the loudest individual most of us know. He was pretty much uninterruptable.

The first speech I remember was after Alan got himself quite severely injured trying to stop a break in at a local Co-op near his house. In the real version our hero had gone to investigate an alarm and discovered two handy lads through the smashed window of the shop, helping themselves to the booze and cigarettes. The getaway car was outside, empty, engine running.

The scene was a village in leafy Leicestershire. It was 3am, there were no buses, no taxis, there is no railway station and there was no traffic. Any normal sane off-duty cop would have done one of two things: Got in the car and driven it off whilst calling the cavalry or nicked the keys and hid nearby on the phone, to direct the troops in.

Not Alan. He's no Marvin Hagler but unfortunately he is braver than is good for him and he decided to wait for them to come out so he could nick them. He lost and got smashed over the head with an iron bar, leaving him with a fractured skull.

These were proper villains and weeks later when they were ambushed by a Regional Crime Squad team, a DS got a broken nose for his trouble as they went down fighting. This was against cops with weapons remember, not a daft lad in his pants.

The Major's version of all this was slightly different and he regaled us with it one evening at a do somewhere. It seemed there had never been any villains....

According to the Major, Alan had in fact gone out to the Co-op only to discover that the alarm had been set off by a couple of thirteen year olds messing about. One of them had tripped and banged the window, setting the sirens blaring.

The other lad, the local vicar's son, a five foot Harry Potter lookalike, who was the best player in the school chess club, moved out of the way as Alan tried to detain them for causing a breach of the peace. Alan fell and banged his head on the pavement. The panicked and now tearful boys called him an ambulance and he was taken to hospital. The end.

I have been the victim on a couple of occasions too. The most memorable one came from a trip to Positano Italy, with Katy, celebrating her fortieth birthday in 2010. We were having a lovely time but the World Cup was on and Katy knew that I knew England were playing while we were there.

I was genuinely prepared to miss my first England World Cup game since my English O'level exam got in the way of the first half hour of England v France in 1982. Katy said it was OK though and that she fancied trawling the shops in the town for some handmade shoes, while I watched the football in a bar. One of the many reasons I love her.

Permission granted, I sat down in a sea front bar which was not at all busy. We were in Italy after all and this was England v Slovenia. The afternoon sunshine was lovely and it was a good setting to have a drink and watch some footy. There were two other blokes within chatting distance. One was an Essex geezer who was decent and friendly. The other was a thin young bloke with an extremely attractive young lady hanging off his arm.

We were sitting about six feet from the TV and in the first few minutes of the game, three or four people came up to the young bloke and asked him for his autograph. I hadn't realised because I don't watch Doctor Who but it was Matt Smith, the actor. Better known to me in 2020 as Prince Philip in The Crown.

To cut a long story short, he was a really nice bloke and I watched the whole game, having a couple of beers with him and the Essex man. I apologised for not knowing he was The Doctor and he laughed and signed a map for three proper fans, my God sons Sam, Ben, and James.

He is, as it turned out, a massive football fan and has played to a reasonable standard.

And that was it unless you were the Major. He regaled the group at that year's trip with another version in which I had gone looking for a TV at night so I could watch the yobbo's sport: football. This, according to the Major, is what really happened:

I found a lovely, expensive restaurant with one TV in the corner which was not switched on.

Even though it was my wife's birthday trip, I insisted we eat there so I could get the TV switched on for the match.

I berated the staff in this beautiful, candlelit setting until they agreed to turn said TV on.

I then yelled loudly, spoiling the romantic atmosphere by calling Rooney a twat repeatedly and cheering when he was substituted. (That bit *was* true earlier)

I spotted Matt Smith, who does not like football, and was trying to have a romantic dinner with his girlfriend

I yelled '*Oi Doctor*' at him continually and then went over and insisted on a photo despite him trying to politely refuse.

And so it goes with The Major.

Anyway, back in 2004, he was on board for the Great Yarmouth trip and he wasn't planning on being quiet.

I drove up to East Midlands Airport to collect another mate, Greg, who had recently transferred from Leicestershire to a Scottish force but still wanted to come on the trip, so he flew down.

Greg is a dog handler and probably one of the best to ever do the job. He is a proud Scot but ended up moving back to England not long afterwards cos he just loves us.

He is one of the better golfers on the trip and he hits the ball a country mile. He is also one of the genuinely nicest blokes you could wish to meet and he would always be near the top of my list of partners when I was sorting the playing order out.

We never played golf on the first day of any of the trips. We usually tried to find something else to do like go to the dogs or horse racing or failing that play cricket or football on the beach. After the abandoned game in Aberystwyth, we found that the beach in Great Yarmouth was much more suited to football.

Unfortunately, whilst one or two of the group like Blackie and particularly Jason, were good footballers, more of them were egg chasers who thought the rules of rugby could be transferred onto the football pitch. The Major in particular, is a big solid unit and a rugby forward.

He spent the game crashing around, with the technique of an elephant, trying to take people out. Suddenly he went too far and missing his intended target, was sent sprawling and looked like he was in some pain. He had obviously pulled something but he is an obstinate hard man and he decided that instead of resting it he would go for a swim in his pants. Eddie went too because, well, why wouldn't he? That's what Eddie does.

That night, playing killer pool in a pub, the Major was clearly in a lot of pain but he was still trying to play it down. In those days, we didn't use buggies in the main competition. It was against tour rules for anyone to have one unless they had a verifiable grievous injury. Broken leg, that kind of thing.

I looked at the Major and told him he could have a buggy or he would not be making it round the course. He turned me down flat. He is a good golfer, off about thirteen but the next day he was shite. He hobbled around, still refusing a buggy and finished sixteenth out of the twenty players. Even I beat him.

I don't remember much more about the golf. I *can* tell you that Robbo won it and he was a popular winner. He had started coming along in Leeds, as a guest of Jon's and we had all taken to him.

I often played the afternoon Stableford competition with him as he lived quite a bizarre life at times and he had us falling about at his tales. This was a great distraction from my appalling game. Robbo used to be a builder and sometimes the builder appears when he is not meant to. He told us about a time when this happened while he was at work.

He was sitting in the back of a police van with a group of officers on some duty or other which involved a lot of waiting around. To relieve the boredom a young, fresh faced officer suggested they play a game. Everyone had to imagine the scenario in which the Russians had launched nuclear missiles and they all had three hours to live. Then, taking it in turns, each had to say how they would spend the three hours. Robbo went first.

'*Right, first I would get off my tits on whisky. Then I'd probably inject some heroin into my eyeballs. Then I'd find the dirtiest likeminded woman I could and we would shag each other's brains out and that's what I would be.......*'

He stopped because they were all looking at him.

'*What?*'

The organiser of the game explained that he was going make sure he got home to see his kids, make the final tearful call to his parents, cuddle his wife, that sort of thing.

'*Oh sorry*' said the builder. '*I misunderstood*'

Despite those stories Robbo couldn't be further from the builder in reality. One of life's true gents. Which was why he was a popular winner in Yarmouth.

At night we found somewhere to eat and have a beer on the pier. The food was about as good as you would expect on a seaside pier, queue up canteen style and long tables with benches.

The overpriced beer was not much better but as we stood there, having now had quite a few, all hell let loose. Suddenly we were being ushered out and Trumpton were on the scene.

Police officers of a certain age refer to the Fire Service simply as *Trumpton.*

Scouse decided to go and ask what was going on and spoke to a fire officer with a couple of bands round his white hat. This chap didn't seem to want to know and was a bit short tempered, just wanting people off the pier quickly. I didn't see it but apparently Scouse identified himself to the bloke to calm him down and assure him it was a professional interest.

And that was it for the time being. It was a fire but it was small and quickly put out. At breakfast I sat next to Scouse and was about to tuck into my fry up when the Major walked in.

'*Oh my God, he's here!*' he shouted, pointing at Scouse. '*I'm surprised you've got the nerve to show your face after embarrassing yourself last night son!*'

He went on, now performing to his breakfast room audience:

'There we were, enjoying a beer when a massive blaze breaks out. Trumpton turn up and quite rightly want everyone out to save life and limb. Not Scouse though. Oh no he's not having that. He whips out the yellow, fluorescent jacket he keeps folded up in his pocket and sticks that on. Up he goes to the head Trumpton bloke and says 'Police! Can I help?'.

'Trumpton looks at the warrant card and says, "that won't put a fire out son, now piss off." How embarrassing. I'd have stayed in bed.'

I had the dubious pleasure of rooming with the Major on several occasions. The thing is, he was a good person to room with because he was immaculately tidy and he was up and out at the crack of dawn, leaving me to have a free run at the facilities just in time for breakfast. And he would make the tea.

I took to the idea of asking him to do an after dinner style speech which usually went down well. He would generally pick a target and one of his stories would unfold. The Matt Smith version of events came out at my expense during one of these speeches.

Professionally, 2003 and 2004 had been largely consumed by a man called Russell.

In early 2002 he had been arrested for the attempted murder of a police officer called Gary. Gary and his sergeant were alerted by a traffic warden to a stolen Audi parked on Ash Street, about a mile from Leicester city centre, on false plates. The alert warden had noticed that the number plates and the tax disc were different. They decided to watch it covertly to see what happened. Before long, Russell and another man approached. The cops emerged but the two men ran off with Gary following Russell and the sergeant going after the other guy.

As he ran along Ash Street, Russell suddenly turned and raised a handgun towards Gary, who juddered to a stop and froze. Russell fired but he missed and immediately turned and carried on running. Gary, understandably now very shaken, didn't follow. He returned to secure the Audi and find his sergeant, who had managed to catch the other man.

The CID took command of the incident, which was treated as an attempted murder. The officer placed in charge was a popular DS called Gareth. Enquiries soon led to Russell and he was arrested and picked out on an identity parade by Gary and one of two council gardeners, a man and a woman, whose van he ran past straight after the shooting. They got involved when they responded to a press appeal. They had seen '*Russell*' discarding clothing in a flower bed but only the woman and Gary positively identified him.

It is fair to say that those involved in the investigation were not very enamoured by the level of senior support they got. Gareth, with two or three DCs, was left to get on with it. When asked for more money on the budget to get some important forensic work done or more staff to complete key actions, one individual was apparently heard to say, '*Well, it was probably only a bloody air pistol*'.

By May of 2003, it was time for the trial. Russell had managed to get bail and was due to surrender himself at court on the allotted Monday morning. The evidence was reasonable but not great. Forensic opportunities had been missed although it must be said that none of this was due to the diligence of Gareth's team. They had done a fantastic job despite the limitations that they were forced to work within.

Through all of this I was not involved at all. I was a DS at a nearby nick, running my own small CID team. On the weekend before the trial, which I was aware was due to start on the Monday, I was in Wales with Katy and her parents.

On the Saturday morning I awoke to find Leicester on the national news. A man had been shot in the leg outside a Spar shop on Evington Road in Leicester. I said to Katy that I would probably get put on that job on Monday as it was on my patch.

I was right. It transpired that the injured party was Russell. He reported that a man called CD had shot him in the leg. This was, he said, because CD, not Russell, was the assailant who had fired at Gary and CD knew that Russell was preparing to grass him up at court. CD was a bad ass gangster who drove a White MG Metro. Russell's girlfriend had been conveniently waiting with him in her VW Beetle, engine running, and was able to whisk him straight to the Leicester Royal Infirmary, only about a mile away.

The new investigation was led by a veteran old SIO, a Detective Superintendent, ex Met Counter Terrorism guy, a heavy smoker, old school type. He was immensely well-respected. A Detective Inspector I knew well and liked, called Graham, was his deputy but he was still running other jobs, including several murders and had to manage this one as well.

As a result, the two people who sorted this enquiry out on a day-to-day basis were two Detective Sergeants: me and a guy called Chris. Chris was way more experienced than me. I learned more from him about being a detective on a big enquiry than any other single person in my career. And he was also very funny. I became the OIC on this enquiry. Naturally, the imminent trial was postponed but perhaps less expected was that Gareth was told he was not to be part of the new investigation. A baffling decision.

We were instantly suspicious that Russell was up to something but the SIO insisted that we investigate properly what Russell and his girlfriend had reported, without prejudice. This was that CD had come up to them outside the Spar on Evington Road, and shot Russell in the leg. Right under a CCTV camera. The shooting was there for all to see but CD was wearing a hood up and his face wasn't visible.

We did do it justice and even arrested a man with the nickname CD but before long we had worked out that the CD we were looking for didn't exist. Russell had staged the shooting and the dash in his girlfriend's car to the LRI, where quickly treated, his injuries were not too serious in the long term.

Russell and his girlfriend were arrested on suspicion of conspiracy to pervert the course of justice. Nick and Grover, the detectives who were to be the interviewing officers came on the dawn raid to get him. Grover, or just 'G' as I usually called him, is a guy who dresses sharply and thinks he is as cool as Samuel L Jackson. Actually, he is not far off and he did once come to a fancy dress party at my house as Elmo, Jackson's character in *Fifty-First State*. He was also the most moisturised man I had ever met. He put more hand cream on than my mother does. He would argue that consequently he never looked his age!

Russell always seemed to be a little put out by Grover. I've never known why. Maybe he didn't like Grover's laid back style, I don't know, but something seemed to irritate him and Grover played up to that. Whatever the case, Russell was fine with me and I took him up to his own bedroom, in his Mum's house, to search it. I made comment on the number of books he had. Without denigrating the criminal population usually arrested by Leicester CID, most of them do not do books. At least, not ones without pictures.

We didn't find much but one thing I did pick up was Russell's own photo, in a printout from a Leicestershire Police intelligence system, that I could see had been printed by a DC who had been on the original investigation. This was to cause me problems later.

In the interview Russell decided not to bother answering any questions. He was shown CCTV of himself 'casing' the shop the week before. It was our case that he could be seen checking out the CCTV system. He wanted a good place to stage the forthcoming performance.

Grover said to him, '*So, who is that at the Spar?*'

'No comment.'

'Come on, it's you, it's quite clear isn't it?'

'No comment.'

'Why don't you just tell me what you were doing there?'

'No comment.'

The enquiry ran on and on as we fully re-investigated the original incident as well. With a proper SIO to report to and a budget to use, we managed to get some excellent forensic evidence which was quite damning for Russell.

Chris and I had a lot of latitude to do what we needed to do. A few enquiries took staff to London and one day we decided we had worked so bloody hard for weeks that we were going to have the next London trip ourselves. As it happened, almost immediately we had to take some exhibits to the Forensic Science Service down there and have a meeting with one of the experts.

The day came and it was a scorcher. We got off the train at St Pancras early for the meeting and walked all the way to the Thames and over Lambeth Bridge to FSS. The scientist had forgotten about the meeting and taken the day off, so we handed the exhibits in and walked out of there about 11am with nothing left to do.

We walked back along the Thames and I asked Chris to hang on while I opened my rucksack. I took off my tie, shirt, trousers and shoes and put on the t-shirt, shorts and flip flops in my bag. He just looked at me. The master detective hadn't thought of that. He called me a knob though.

We then went in two or three pubs before ending up in Covent Garden at a place called The Cove, where you could get a good pint of beer – not lager – and a pie from a choice of about fifty sorts. We were tucking into the pies, mid-afternoon when two familiar faces walked in. Mike, suitor of the broken armed girl in Bath was one of them. He was a DC from the same CID area as me and he was with his DS, a guy called Albert.

We spent the next few hours drinking until they decided they needed to catch the 5pm train as they had reserved seats. Chris and I decided we'd go for that train with them. We made it to St Pancras and got on to a carriage awash with little reserved tickets sticking out the top of the seats.

Luckily, Chris and I found two seats with no tickets in front of a table and sat down. Mike and Albert's seats had the little tickets in the top but there was a man sitting in one of them. The following conversation then ensued as we watched:

Albert *'Excuse me mate but we have these seats reserved, would you mind moving please?'*

Man *'I would but they're all reserved so I'm staying. Sit somewhere else'*

Albert *'I don't think so matey. You need to move. They're our seats'*

Mike *'Albert!'*

Albert *'I'm handling it Mike'*

Man *'I'm not telling you again. I'm not moving now piss off'*

Mike *'Albert, wait!'*

Albert *'Mike will you just shut up. This twat is going to move or I'll just get a member of staff to move him'*

Man *'What did you call me big mouth?'*

Mike *'Albert!!'*

Albert *'What?!'*

Mike *'We're on the wrong carriage'*

Chris and I were on the floor.

Albert had a habit of saying the wrong thing. One day in the CID office he was berating Darren for something Darren had said that Albert thought was wrong. As he was talking, I answered the ringing phone on his desk because he was getting into such a rant that he hadn't noticed it.

He was just shouting *'That's exactly the sort of thing my stupid idiotic fucking wife would say!'* as I was saying hello to the same wife, who incidentally wears the trousers in their house.

I passed the phone over and the whole office heard Albert assure her that he would definitely not be going for the drink he had just told us he was going for in the station bar at 4pm. He was, he said, definitely going straight home.

Back to the job, we had no witnesses who could say Russell had arranged his own shooting and still only the two identifications of him by Gary and the gardener for the original crime.

We ended up charging him and his mate with Conspiracy to Rob too. The Audi was not only on stolen plates, it was also equipped with a scanner tuned to police and security company frequencies. And let us not forget the gun. We thought that they were going to hit a cash in transit van or a high value static target somewhere. We knew it was a weak case though.

The main event was the attempted murder, supported by the pervert the course of justice charge, handling of the stolen Audi and possession of the firearm. When we charged Russell with '*Pervert the Course*' for derailing his trial with the leg shooting, he was calm about it and asked if he could have a cigarette. None of the custody staff wanted to supervise him smoking in the exercise yard so I said I would do it.

Outside he asked me '*I suppose you lot will be going for a beer to celebrate, won't you?*'

'*No*' I said. '*We have got nothing to celebrate yet. We will if you get convicted. We think you're guilty and we are just doing our jobs.*'

We carried on talking for the next ten minutes and then I took him back. The rest of the investigation, which lasted for over a year, was the hard yards of getting all of the forensic evidence, the phone evidence and the mass of circumstantial evidence sorted.

Personally, my life was about to change forever. In December 2003 I walked into the office on a Monday morning and when asked if I'd had a good weekend I responded as follows:

'*Yes, but I think it was the single most bizarre weekend of my life. Not only have we found out that Katy is pregnant but we had a scan and she is halfway through. We had no idea!*'

Katy used to have a condition that meant we would probably not be able to have kids but when she was due to have an MRI scan the previous Thursday for a back injury, they made her take a pregnancy test as normal procedure. *We could not believe the result.* We thought it was wrong and we told nobody. To sort it out, we paid for a test on the Sunday at a private hospital.

We met a nice Australian chap, a gynaecological consultant no doubt earning more that Sunday morning than your average police officer did in a month.

With a very relaxing manner the Aussie settled Katy onto the couch and smeared her tummy liberally with a blue gel. She sucked in her breath at the coldness and we smiled at each other. The screen flickered into life and I stared into the grey, black and whiteness of it all trying to make sense of a shape.

The Aussie was first to speak.

'Well that's a baby.'

'Oh God,' said Katy. *'I knew as soon as the screen came on.'*

'Fucking hell' was my contribution.

They both looked at me.

'Can you estimate the age of the baby?' asked Katy.

'No,' I replied. *'I wouldn't know where to start.'*

Her look told me two things: You know I am talking to the doctor. Shut up.

He was looking at me strangely again but he answered Katy.

'Looking at the measurements, its twenty weeks.'

'That's halfway' said Katy incredulously. *'That's four and a half months, isn't it?'*

'Correct' he replied.

'Fucking hell.' I said.

They both looked at me again.

Four and half months later we had a beautiful daughter and as I write, she is seventeen and more beautiful still.

Back to work then. We got on fantastically well with Adrian our barrister and in fact I still meet up with him for a beer now and again, after he got in touch a few years ago and invited me to Lords as his guest as an MCC member. Chris and I used to have a lot of fun with him, often because he would set a date for *'a con'* (conference) with us and then change it at the last minute.

Adrian was an ex-cop, a City of London DI, who had changed careers a few years earlier so there was a natural connection. In the lead up to the trial in the autumn of 2004 Russell tried to get bail. We got some intelligence that if he got it, he would be skipping the country to the Caribbean.

The source of the intel was extremely sensitive and at the bail hearing we didn't use it for fear of being asked for more detail. We thought there was no way the judge at Leicester Crown Court would give bail to a man accused of shooting a Leicestershire police officer. Even though the custody time limits, which govern how long he could ordinarily be kept in prison on bail, had expired.

We were right and his bail was refused. Then Russell surprised us by quickly appealing the decision at the High Court, where things didn't go well. Bail was granted by one of the Lords, provided the police could verify the suitability of one of three bail addresses his lawyers had put forward.

We took our time checking these and lodged an unprecedented appeal of the High Court decision – right there in the High Court. We knew that we would have to reveal our intelligence source but applied to do it in private.

Chris and I went to the Royal Courts of Justice for this hearing and we took along the force intelligence unit inspector. This was actually Rich, who had been the young pissed up DC who set fire to the toilet roll in the Indian restaurant in Whitby six years earlier.

In a hearing from which all of the defence team were excluded, Rich provided the details on where the intelligence log had come from which told us that Russell was planning to run for the hills as soon as he got out.

The judge told us in no uncertain terms that this was a difficult one for him. He said that the time limits had expired and he had never overturned a decision like this from a 'brother high court judge' before. He left the court to consider his decision, no doubt whistling up 'the old boy network' for opinion.

I went out into the corridor, where sat Stephen Coward QC, one of the most eminent criminal barristers in the country. Way more experienced than Adrian. He was quite chatty although I was alive to the fact he was trying to see what he could get out of me. It was apparent that they thought the leak was from the prison Russell was in and that Rich, with a new sharp haircut and a cheap suit, was a prison officer. I didn't confirm or deny that one and as we all know, this meant that they thought I had confirmed it.

Anyway, wherever the judge went for advice was the right place for us. He overturned the bail decision and Russell was banged back up. The trial was on for November.

We went for a coffee with Adrian. He was really pleased and said, '*We'll have a con next Wednesday, your place, 10am.*' Chris burst out laughing.

'*What?*' said Adrian.

'Nothing' I said, *'except that every time you arrange one you change it so we won't bother writing it down.'*

'Fuck off!' he said, *'The CPS think you're all wankers anyway*!'

In what was my first big (six week) trial I found that I loved it. There was a lot to do and it seemed to be going our way despite a sticky moment. One thing we lost straight away was Russell's girlfriend on the conspiracy charge. The judge felt the evidence was not there and he let her go. I had no problem with that. In all probability, she was just doing what she was told.

The sticky moment was not that though. Russell's team applied to have all the evidence of the identification parades excluded. Gary had picked him out of a line up on a different day to the gardener and we had anticipated they might try this.

The obvious tactic was to say that as a policeman working in the local area, Gary had been tipped off as to the identity of the person who had been arrested and had looked at photos to see what he looked like.

We got that wrong. They actually used the exhibit I had picked up in Russell's house against us. The photograph of him which had been printed by one of the DCs on the job had, he said, been left lying around the ID suite by someone so he pocketed it. Their case was that if he had seen it, so could Gary. It was utter bollocks but His Honour Judge Stokes went with it and excluded Gary's identification of Russell.

They then tried to get the evidence of the gardener excluded too. They appeared to have had her followed and established that she sometimes popped into a Co-op in Evington on her way to work in the morning. Russell lived in Evington. The implication was that she had seen him in there and had picked him out because he looked familiar, no malice, just a mistake.

This time Stokes told them to clear off.

Gary's evidence was compelling and the jury were clearly with him. Stephen Coward QC tried to make something out of the fact that Gary had not apparently noticed what the QC felt was a quite distinctive skin contrast on Russell's face. Gary pointed out that at the time, he was distracted by the small matter of a gun being aimed at his head.

Ultimately Russell hung himself when he gave evidence, by coming up with a new and even more fanciful story which beggared belief. As the trial neared its end, on Friday 12th November, I was told of new intelligence from the same source that had prevented his bail. This information said that Russell was planning to try to escape from court.

In those days, only one court dock in Leicester Crown was completely secure, with a top on it. We were not in that court as it was being used for a high profile murder trial which warranted a detachment of support officers including armed officers in and around the court building. This was the trial of those accused of shooting the two young Shakespeare sisters plus others with a machine pistol in Birmingham in January 2003.

That situation really helped us. Or so I thought. All we had left was the judge's summing up so I went and spoke to Julie, the support inspector on duty that day and asked for a couple of her officers to assist. If she could just put two officers by the main courtroom entry airlock we'd have it covered. Her officers were obviously in full PPE and carried batons and rigid cuffs, which we in the courtroom were not allowed to do.

All we needed was that main door guarded. If he tried to run through the judge's door behind the bench, he'd find himself looking down the sharp and of a Heckler & Kock carbine as the firearms teams were patrolling the corridors behind all of the courts.

Julie wanted to know where the intel had come from. I told her I couldn't disclose that but I was satisfied with the provenance of it. She said she considered it gossip and that there was a risk that every high profile criminal might try to escape if they could. She refused point blank to assist.

Stokes's summing up of the case started and was going well for us until he cautioned the jury about a cross contamination issue that had arisen on a forensic exhibit. He told them that they needed to consider whether the evidence we were relying on was tainted at all.

As he said this, I was sitting to the left side of the dock, with Chris next to me on my right. Alongside him was our DI, Graham. On my left was a police officer from the HOLMES team and Gareth, the original DS on the shooting. We had tipped him off to come in for these closing stages because he still had a lot invested in the outcome. We couldn't see Russell because the sides of the dock were opaque and well over six feet high.

If ever there was a moment for Russell not to do what he did next, this was it. The judge was just making a great point for the defence, albeit not a correct one in our view.

Suddenly there was a shout of '*No don't!*' and a banging and clattering from the dock. Russell leapt over the top and into the courtroom, running past the jury and up onto the judge's bench, by a gate on the right.

Chris, Graham and I all followed him. Gareth went through the gate on the left. Before we could get to him, he had the judge by his sash and was ragging him about. Russell was a very fit and powerful man and he could have done the much older Stokes a proper injury, he could have smashed a fist straight though his face before we got there.

He didn't though, he just kept shaking him about and as he did this he shouted, '*I've got previous convictions!*'

We all dived on top of him, Graham, Chris and I getting in each other's way and Gareth quite sensibly coming from the other side. Gareth managed force his body in between the judge and Russell and got a grip on his right arm. Russell may have been strong but so was Gareth; as a young man he had been a GB standard javelin thrower, in the top three or four in the country.

I shoved my shoulder into Russell's front and tried to help Gareth get a lock on his right arm while Graham and Chris worked on the left. Russell, meanwhile, carried on shouting:

'*All I want is a fair trial! I'm an Englishman!*'

And then seemingly directed at the judge he said, '*It was worth it just to see the look on your face!*'

I said to him '*What are you doing fella? Pack it in*'

He shouted, '*Get off me. I'm not trying to escape*'

At that moment in rushed a Tactical Support Group (TSG) officer called Alistair, who had been alerted by someone pushing a panic button. He got some cuffs on Russell and then as more of his colleagues ran in to help, he got him up and off to the cells.

The fun and games were not quite over yet and it was another mistake by the police to blame for that. Once he had calmed down, the judge naturally wondered about the security situation. He knew there were a lot of police officers in the building and wondered why with all that, it took four CID officers to come to his aid, without any handcuffs or weapons.

The shift had changed over in the afternoon so by the time Stokes summoned the duty support inspector it was a different one. The inspector took his own sergeant with him, to get Julie's bollocking. Nothing wrong with that you would think. The defence thought otherwise.

A couple of hours later the court was reconvened. Russell was brought up in handcuffs with extra security guards. The judge started by thanking us for coming to his assistance. The jury were not there at this point because Mr Coward QC wanted to apply for the trial to be halted.

He made the case that what the jury had seen and heard was so prejudicial that they could not now reach a fair verdict. Then, he told the judge that he had been appalled to find out that the sergeant who had visited him in his chambers with the duty inspector, without any representative from the defence present, was a prosecution witness.

He was right too. It was the sergeant who had been with Gary on the day of the shooting in 2002. He had given evidence in the first week of the trial. What is more, I had seen him walking towards the court, knowing he was on security duty but not realising where he was going. If only I had asked, I could have stopped it. But I didn't, and this was now forming part of Mr Coward's submission.

Adrian came back at the judge with all the reasons why, in his view, Stephen Coward was wrong. It was a good submission from the ex-DI. More measured than Mr Coward's manufactured outrage. The judge went off to consider it all and then came back hard in our favour. He said that if he aborted this trial a bad precedent would be set. Every time a defendant in a dock thought a trial was going wrong, they would know exactly how to stop it.

The show goes on, he said, and he told Russell the issue of the contempt of court was going to be dealt with by another judge.

Stokes finished his summing up on the following Monday and sent the jury out. On Tuesday 16th November they were back to give their verdict. I looked at the foreman and thought he looked like a mate of mine called Rog. I was shaking like a shitting dog. So was Chris, although he was telling me to calm down and had been here many times before.

The first count was the handling of the stolen Audi used on the day. We knew if we got that, we would be in the game. I thought I could see my shirt moving where my heart was beating.

The foreman took a breath, '*Guilty*' he said. The next count was attempted murder. '*Guilty*.'

No need for the alternative count of attempted GBH. The jury obviously felt that if you fire a gun at person's head you are not hoping to just wing them. The intention is to kill. I gripped Chris's arm and looked at Gareth. He just exhaled for about two minutes. Justice for him and all the shit he had put up with. Air pistol my arse!

He was also found guilty of the possession of a firearm with intent to resist arrest and the separate count of conspiracy to pervert the course of justice. We never did charge the shooter in that conspiracy although we were fairly sure on who it was. We just didn't have the evidence and there was little appetite from the CPS to go on with it.

Sentencing was a few days later and Stokes warned the court before he announced it, that this was a very grave crime and everyone should be prepared for a big number. He hit Russell with twenty years plus concurrent sentences of two years for the car and thirteen for the gun. He then added a consecutive four years for perverting the course of justice. Twenty-four years.

Twenty-four years which that afternoon became twenty five and a half when he got eighteen months from Judge Hammond for leaping out of the dock.

The conspiracy to rob was due to be tried next but we knew the case was weak. We had still never figured out what they were going to do that day and the CPS offered no evidence. It was all over after eighteen months.

I have hated some of the people I have dealt with and for trying to kill Gary I should detest Russell but I never did. I always found him easy to get on with and quite eloquent. That said, his plans and stories to try to get away with things were a bit too fanciful and great job that we all did, he was partly responsible for his own downfall.

After the sentencing, the judge announced that the SIO, along with Chris, Gareth and I would all be getting his commendation. Russell's mate from the original day in the Audi was in court and on hearing this he shouted, '*Lying bastards!*'

Russell never did any of that sort of thing. He was released from prison a few years ago, having done a good chunk of the sentence. I have no idea where he is now but I did hear, from Gary of all people, that he might be involved in community work, trying to improve some young lives perhaps. If he is, all credit to him. I have often wondered about asking him what they were actually up to that day. I don't suppose I ever will. I doubt very much he would want to shake hands and have a chat, so I guess we'll never know.

Time for more golf trips.

Weston Super Mare 2005

I TRAVELLED to this one with The Power, in his BMW, which as it turned out could pass anything else on the road. I had my eyes closed for most of it. The Power was a DC at the time, a transferee from Surrey Police who came to my CID office and lived in the same village as me.

At some point he took and passed the full police advanced driving course. I never worked out how because I never saw him drive for more than a mile within the speed limit of whichever road he was on. I was happy to welcome him on his first trip if for no other reason than he was another contender for last place.

On this trip, Boris was back. He was a career detective who specialised in complicated frauds and was particularly good at them. Investigating them I mean, not committing them. When he retired, he came straight back as a civilian investigator specialising in that area of crime.

He was also a decent golfer, although it was hard to pin him down on his handicap. And he is as tight as the proverbial duck's arse.

He was not originally meant to be on the trip but someone dropped out at the last minute and offered his place up to the highest bidder. We had all paid £150. Boris beat him down to £75 for two nights bed and breakfast, three rounds of golf, one lunch and a contribution to the prize fund.

The first night, some of the boys stayed out until not long before getting up time. They managed to find a casino and got hammered playing roulette and blackjack. One was Lee, who came on nearly all the trips. He is an outstanding cricketer and a decent all round sportsman who usually did very well on the trips, often in the top four without ever winning it. Naturally, Blackie and Alan were with him in the casino.

The next day Lee looked absolutely shocking. He was as white as a sheet. I didn't quite expect him to do what he did around the back of the pro shop but I was not going to get in his way. I just hope nobody slipped in it. In the *Texas Scramble* that morning, Alan looked just as bad but at lunchtime he had a beer and he suddenly perked up.

The course, a links with views out over the Bristol Channel, was one of the best and certainly one of the toughest we ever played. It was lovely hot sunny weather but whilst beautifully looked after, the ground was rock hard and the ball flew all over the place off the surface.

Not wanting to bore you with handicaps again but just to explain that a player scoring thirty-six points in a *Stableford* match is putting up a great score and has an excellent chance of winning the tournament.

On this course, in these conditions I felt there was no way anyone was going to get thirty-six points. It looked like one where a good score was thirty-three or thirty-four and that should be enough to take the trophy and the green jacket. I had acquired one just like the one famously used in the US Masters tournament.

A rejuvenated Alan went out like a rocket and immediately proved me wrong. On the ninth green he rolled a putt in to get to twenty points and he was only halfway round.

Then, to use the place name in Cockney Rhyming Slang, he started having a right *Weston Super.*

In between the ninth and tenth holes there is a toilet block. In some ways it was nice for him to be able to use a real convenience rather than have another shit in a bush. When he came out though he looked different. Alan, a few pounds lighter and with the kids dropped off at the pool was the epitome of the biblical Samson, shorn of his locks.

For the remaining nine holes he took every opportunity to lie down. We were playing slightly quicker than the four in front and he was literally sleeping between holes as we waited on each tee. He got four more points over the nine holes and finished seventeenth, beating me by two.

Jon brought up the rear. His fifteen points was around the kind of score the person in last place normally got. I have had less and losers sometimes had more, but it's in that ballpark. I have only got written stats from 2004 to 2018 and in that time I came last three times. A good tournament for me was finishing halfway down the scoreboard but usually I didn't quite manage that.

Two of my last place finishes were technicalities though as there was a player each time who '*retired hurt*' whilst on a lower score than me. If a player retired hurt I would not give them the prize for coming last. I was determined that to get it, you had to stay the course.

One person, Gordon, who came on eight or nine trips over the years, walked off twice with injuries, but on the occasions where he *did* make it round, he came last every single time.

Gordon was not a bad footballer. In particular he was a decent goalkeeper, who played a lot of local league games. He was a fair cricketer as well. For some reason he just could not do golf. He was the worst player we ever had on the trips but boy did he keep coming back for more.

In seven trips between 2004 and 2013 he scored a *total* of twenty-seven points. He had the last laugh though. I never wanted the loser to be too embarrassed, so I always made sure the 'wooden spoon' was a good prize.

After his first couple of trips, it got to the stage where I would just call Gordon before the tournament and ask him what he wanted for coming last. He had wedges, putters, woods and all sorts off me. It did occur to me to wonder if he was really a good player and was secretly assembling a free set of clubs and using them to better effect elsewhere.

He wasn't. He really was that crap.

Back to Weston in 2005. Boris ended up taking the title with thirty-five points so I wasn't far out with my guess at a winning score.

Jason and Robbo both scored thirty-four and had to be separated by a countback rule, Jason coming second because his back nine was superior to Robbo's. There is a reason for me telling you that bit. Stick with me.

After the prizes were dished out, normally done once we were all changed for the night with a beer in hand, we headed off towards the fleshpots of Weston. Despite first appearances we found a nice bar to sit outside of, split over two levels.

During each tournament there were always a few things to win. You could win the overall *Stableford* (the main event), you could be in the winning team in the *Texas Scramble* and you could also win the *Longest Drive* and *Nearest the Pin* prizes, placed on two different, specific holes.

Then there is the dubious honour of being '*The Worst off the First*'. This prize is handed out to celebrate the best comedy tee shot in the morning. Someone once won it by hitting his own foot with the ball.

Eddie also ran a sweep on the golf, like a Grand National sweep but instead of horses we all drew someone else's name from the hat and he paid out on the top three in the afternoon *Stableford* tournament. He did a National Lottery bonus ball competition too. Eddie likes a competition and a bet.

At Weston, having paid half of what everyone else had paid, Boris won the *Stableford*, the *Texas Scramble*, the bonus ball draw and came second on the sweep, having drawn Jason's name. He netted a haul of about £65 in cash, £75 in Next vouchers and nine quality golf balls.

That evening, I walked up to the bar with Blackie, Alan and the Power. We saw Boris standing with Darren, his good mate. Blackie immediately pointed out to him that he should be getting the organiser (me) a beer in and while he was at it, one for the rest of our foursome, given that he was up on the whole cost of his trip. Boris was having none of it. He was in a round with Darren, he said. Even Darren looked embarrassed and I think he got me a beer but Boris was devoid of any shame.

Then the controversy started. PD, never one to miss a possible rule breach, especially after finishing eighth, brought it to my attention. I summoned Blackie, as I normally would. Him and PD were my go-to people for the regulations. I can barely remember what kind of socks to wear at most clubs.

It seemed there had been an issue over a wrongly played ball and with the agreement of the group he was in, Boris had accepted a *one shot* penalty. Blackie and PD pointed out, in the bar, that the correct penalty is *two shots*. This would have placed Boris on thirty-four points with Robbo and Jason and in fact relegated him to third as both the others both had better back nines than him.

He did, to be fair to him, offer to surrender the prize but I made the decision, unpopular with some, that the penalty had been agreed at the time and cards handed in and accepted, so the result stood. Boris's name went on the trophy.

I did get a slight portion of retribution for the tightness though. On the way back, Boris needed a lift home so having the whole of the back of the Power's BMW estate free, we offered. The Power told me we would need fuel. His Lewis Hamilton drive down may have got us past every other car on the road but he didn't go past many petrol pumps. I quietly told him not to go anywhere near the kiosk once he had filled up. He pumped in about half a tank and I turned to Boris and told him what the deal was.

'OOOH noooo mate that's not fair!' was the initial response but he ended up laughing and paying up. He stretched to a bag of sweets for the journey too. I didn't realise that his tightness would be revisiting me again a couple of years later but more of that when we get there.

Professionally I had opted for a career change and joined the Special Branch Department. It was to be a short fifteen month move before the lure of murder investigation took me to Major Crime. The event of note happened about a month into my time there, just after the Weston Super Mare trip. It was the London terrorist attacks on three tube trains and a double decker bus on 7th July of that year. As with tragedies like Dunblane and 9/11 it is one of those moments when you remember where you were when you heard about it.

East Midlands Airport, where I was based, was hardly a main hub for the investigation but we did have a very heightened security situation. The following year, while I was still at the airport, we had another raising of the security threat level to *'critical'*. This was after a new alert about liquids being used as explosives and was what inspired the current restrictions we all now routinely accept, on taking liquids airside in an airport.

As with 7/7 we found ourselves with extra officers in the port, some in plain clothes, some not but mostly they were armed. One of these teams was a group of about five Leicestershire firearms officers led by Graham, who had been one of the instructors on my initial firearms course back in 1992.

I always got on really well with him. For a start he was a fellow Leeds fan. For some reason he always called me Shultz instead of just Shutts like most people did. I've never known why.

One day I was in the office when Graham rang. He asked if there was somewhere his team of armed uniformed cops could have a lunch break, out of public view. They had all got meal deals of sandwiches, crisps and a drink from Boots and wanted a sit down. I told him to come through airport security and meet me airside and I would show him into a suite of rooms they could sit in. Ten minutes later he rang me back. He was less than amused. He told me what had happened.

Graham had led the team up to the security arches. They all put their food bags in a grey tray to go through the scanner and they stepped forward. They couldn't be searched because they were carrying weapons that it would be unlawful for a civilian security guard to possess or seize.

The security guard stopped Graham and pointed to his '*Ribena*' drink in the tray.

'*You can't take that through mate*' he said.

'*Why not?*' asked Graham.

'*Rules,*' said the man. '*No liquids airside. You can make a bomb with that you know.*'

'*Hang on,*' said Graham. '*I've got a Heckler and Koch MP5 carbine here with a twenty round mag fitted, plus one up the spout and another two mags on my leg.*'

'*Yeah that's fine,*' said the man, deadpan.

'*And I've got a Glock pistol with thirteen rounds in the mag, one up the spout, a taser, some nasty fucking spray that makes your eyes sting and a big baton. What about them?*'

'Yeah they are all OK. Oh, and tell your mate at the back with the dog to just come straight through'

'I will. But not the Ribena?'

'No. Not the Ribena.'

That's when Graham called me.

'Is he taking the piss Schultz?' he asked.

I said no he wasn't and not to try having a joke with the guy because he wouldn't get it. At least not for a couple of days. I told him to go back round the corner and put the Ribena in his pocket, then try again and they would let him through.

You couldn't make it up.

Bournemouth 2006

2006 MARKED a sea change for us when I discovered Meyrick Park in Bournemouth. For the first time we had a site where we could park the cars up and leave them for the duration; there was a big swimming pool with jacuzzi, sauna and steam room; a nice balcony to use at the side of the bar and the first tee was about twenty yards from the front door of the accommodation block. This was a wooden lodge with seventeen nice clean rooms over two floors of odd-shaped corridors and annexes.

All that and it was also walkable to the beach and the town centre.

That first hole is probably the hardest opener we ever had on the trips. It is a par three measuring 220 yards. It starts with a steep drop into a gully that you have to walk through before climbing up the even steeper far side, with a bank of woodland peering down on the inviting right of the fairway. The green is set way back in a little horseshoe of banked rough. I never, ever, hit that green with my tee shot. Getting down in five was a positively peachy start for me and most of the others with plus twenty-one handicaps.

The proximity of the rooms to the first tee was not always appreciated. Like the time I was woken at 3am by Alan and Blackie playing nearest the pin on the first, whilst arseholed. I wouldn't mind but Alan was hitting the green regularly, which he rarely did when sober.

On this first Bournemouth trip Alan made the rare and welcome offer to drive, so off we went in this purple Rover contraption he had at the time. I can't remember who I roomed with, probably the Power or the Major. By this time Alan and Blackie always roomed together and could be seen after a late night out, sitting up in side by side twin beds like Morecambe and Wise, having a cup of tea.

Cricket on the beach became a regular occurrence in Bournemouth over the years. As did the Major and Eddie going for a swim. The course too, was a hit. It was always in fair nick, sometimes a bit dry but always a challenge.

One hole though, had a green which backed onto some woods. After our first round some of the boys reported seeing suspicious looking characters lurking in the woods. All men.

Before the second round we established through a bloke in the pro shop that the woods were above a primary school and the people in the bushes were perverts, pleasuring themselves, watching little kids run about. He said the police knew about this and sometimes turned up to deal with them.

Robbo decided a less subtle approach than '*move along now*' was required. Leading by example, he dug out a half dozen of his grubbiest golf balls, just in front of the green at this hole. Sure enough, there was a scuttling of moving weirdos and Robbo let fly. The scuttling got faster and a few of us ended up having a go at '*twat the paedo*' without ever being sure if we hit one.

Boris took the honours for the second year running with a bang on his handicap thirty-six points. At least this year he had to pay full price. Lee, Robbo and PD were, as usual, in amongst it with good scores in the thirties but this year so was Eddie, the famous bugle sounding all the way round to his fourth place.

I should have taken that as a warning of things to come but I did not. Eddie is a top bloke but top golfer? Nah. A lesson I would learn a few years later.

On a good night out, we went to quite a few bars before someone suggested Spearmint Rhino. I felt that the safest place to be was with Eddie. We arrived during the club happy hour and were knocking back bottles of beer for £1 a go. Half the lads were shitting themselves at the thought of their wives finding out they had been in a strip club. I just stuck with Eddie.

The trip was a massive success and I started to wonder if I should keep up the policy of never going to the same place twice.

The next day after the friendly Friday round Alan and I set off for home. We got about twenty minutes up the road in the purple pig before he pulled over and declared himself too tired to go on. So, I ended up driving home anyway, in a crap little car.

Bournemouth 2007

IN SEPTEMBER 2006 I had left Special Branch and joined the Major Crime Unit. Back to my old stamping ground at Braunstone and I loved it. I was reunited with Baras, as the other DS on my new team. We had joined the police together and done everything from entrance exam to medical to being in Class 7/87 at training school together. Well, we didn't do the mile and a half run together because he was a former Royal Navy middle distance runner but I could at least see him for the whole of the race, on the oval at Abbey Park in Leicester.

After that though we had gone our separate ways and never worked together. That all changed in 2006. Added to which he made his golf trip debut in 2007.

I had decided we would go back to Bournemouth because it had been such a success. The other reason was because I came close to not organising a trip at all after the birth of child number two, my fantastic little boy this time, in June. In the end I quickly organised a return to Meyrick Park in the August, after Katy gave me the green light for three days off nappy duty.

Boris announced that he wouldn't be able to come back and defend his title though. I feared the worst from his tightness and was immediately proved right when he turned up in our office with the trophy. I had bought the trophy after the first two or three trips and had it engraved with the names of the winners up to that point.

From then on, the winner was told to pay for their own name to be engraved and then to hand it back to me just before or at the start of the trip.

Of course, Scrooge turned up with the trophy minus his name, as I had anticipated. I'd like to say he made up a whining excuse as to why he had failed to do it but he didn't bother. A man without shame and skin thicker than a Rhino is not troubled by such trivialities.

I stopped him as he was about to turn and run. A good mate of his was one of my team DCs, Andy. He was in the office and Boris knew Andy would give him proper grief for being such a tight-wad, so he was keen to get out. I pointed out that he had failed to return the green jacket.

The initiated will know that the US Masters, one of the four golfing 'majors' of each year, always results in the winner being given a green jacket – a blazer really – which is slipped onto his shoulders by the previous winner. We decided to copy this and I bought a forty inch chest version, in the proper colour – British Racing Green - that each winner had to wear for the evening.

After a couple of years, it became apparent that as your average cop is somewhat larger than a forty inch, we needed a bigger jacket. So I tasked my Mum & Dad to find me one, with a £10 budget and they came up trumps. We got a forty-four blazer in new condition from Age Concern in Ashby-de-la-Zouch. Boris had taken this jacket home in 2006 and obviously forgotten to bring it back with the trophy.

'*Come on Boris,*' I said. '*Last year I paid to have the trophy engraved after you won in Weston and I will have to do the same again. At least do the decent thing and make sure the jacket is spick and span when you return it.*'

He agreed that he would.

A couple of weeks later he came in with the jacket in a cellophane wrapper complete with dry cleaning ticket. I could not believe it. He said he was sorry about the trophy, so he thought he had better have the jacket cleaned.

When he had left, I was still a bit suspicious, so I took the jacket out of the bag and looked at it. It was fine. All clean and tidy and I felt a bit guilty. Andy had watched all this with interest. He knew Boris better than anyone. He got up and looked at the jacket, which I had put back its bag.

'Are you sure it's OK skip?' he said. *'It's really not like that tight bastard to pay for anything.'*

'Andy, sometimes you have to give credit where it's due. He's even had it dry cleaned,' I said.

Andy had a couple of looks at the jacket and seemed to accept that it was what it was. Then about two hours later he suddenly jumped up and walked quickly over to where I had hung it on the office clothes rail.

He grabbed the dry cleaning ticket off the top and shouted out:

'The tight bastard! He's done it again!'

'Done what?' said one of the team.

'This!' he shouted, pointing at the jacket and the ticket. *'This is a Sketchley ticket for a fucking tie from 1993. They went bust about eight years ago!'*

A few years later Andy was Boris's best man and told the story to his friends and family. Boris asked me a couple of times over the years, to let him know if anyone dropped out at the last minute but no-one did and he never came back again.

He remains the only person to make a profit out of his overall attendance on the Central Area Golf Trip.

The 2007 trip was the one where PD finally managed to win it. He was often in the top three and never lower than eighth because he was a proper golfer. See previous entries. In 2007 he knew he was playing well. The problem was the course was in lovely nick and lots of other people were in form. We knew the course a little bit better now too and I favoured a high scoring contest.

Alan and I held court as the Handicap Committee, from the Meyrick Park jacuzzi, the night before. Lee got cut a couple of shots just for cavilling. This was a term the Major used to write on his list of reasons to fine the staff in the CID when he was a DS, although he could never spell it.

In the event PD scored thirty-eight points in a high scoring field. The people he was most afraid of were Jason, because of his lifelong gripe that Jason was a bandit and Blackie because he knew that if the

2003 Blackie turned up it could be game over. Neither of those played their best game though and a few other names began to emerge as contenders for the crown. Baras showed some form in a joint fourth place finish with the Major.

The other class act was Thomo. He was a Chief Superintendent during one of my DI postings and he was that rare senior officer who comes to find you to tell you things and offer support rather than summon you to his office. Everyone liked Thomo. One reason was for his Frank Bruno laugh: '*Hurggh, Hurggh*!'

The Power, having debuted in 2005, became another long standing tripper. Unfortunately, he emerged from this trip with the nickname *'Golden Gloves'* assigned by Alan. On one tricky hole he found himself deep in the trees with Scouse.

It seemed impossible that either would find their balls but suddenly there was a shout from The Power of, *'found it!'* followed by the ball sailing through a canopy of vegetation akin to that navigated by the Chindits in Burma in 1942 and landing in the middle of the fairway with just a wedge left to the green.

Scouse seemed to get out very easily too but benefitted slightly less and reacted more violently to the ribbing, so the Power retained the Golden Gloves title and took most of the shit. The subject still comes up now and again.

Scouse was also responsible for a wind up on the unsuspecting PD. Knowing that PD was in with thirty-eight points and that Greg, our intrepid dog handler, had oh so nearly caught him with thirty-seven, he decided to have some fun.

He had overheard PD on the phone just before he walked into the leisure club, talking to someone, saying, *'I've won it. Finally, I've actually won it.'*

He seemed, quite rightly, elated at having captured the title that had eluded him so long until Scouse joined him in the steam room and let him know that Greg had pipped him at the post.

Scouse and I kept it to ourselves until the presentations and it was only when PD saw Greg get second place that the penny dropped. He deserved the win, just because he was so often the *actual* best player there and had previously lost out to the handicap system in the same way that Blackie had in Bath in 2003.

Blackpool 2008

WE HAD a chat and decided that we needed to move on from Bournemouth for a year. The old Charles Street CID golf trip that ours had succeeded way back in 1998 had once been to the De Vere Hotel, Heron's Reach in Blackpool and we decided to give it a go. It was certainly a good standard of accommodation and it meant that, as with Meyrick Park, nobody had to drive anywhere, once we had arrived.

I had last been to Blackpool in 1992 for my stag do. Thanks to my bargain hunter best man, Matt, we ended up in a ramshackle bed and breakfast; eight of us in two rooms. I am trying to think of a kind description and having given it some thought and toned it down a bit I'll just say it was a fucking shithole. We put our bags in our rooms and were about to go to the pub when the landlord said he wanted a word. He took me, Matt and another member of the group to a large basement room which had its own bar and was decked out like a nightclub.

He then proceeded to tell us he could organise a private party for us with girls and anything else we needed. We declined and left quickly going for a pint at the Blackpool Police Club, as we had parked our minibus there and told them we would.

Inside we found a proper old fashioned police social club with two snooker tables, dart boards, a juke box and a good old crowd having a beer. One of them asked Matt where we were staying and Matt gave the name of the place.

The way the story goes, as soon as the words had left Matt's lips, the balls on the snooker tables stopped rolling, the juke box shuddered to a halt, the clocks stopped ticking and one of the cops whispered, '*Where?!*'

It turned out that the landlord had been busted in a drugs raid and there had been an armed siege at the place, to name but two of the many incidents to have taken place there over the years.

Thankfully, he must have decided not to mess us about and all that happened to me was that I ended the night traditionally naked on the sea front, handcuffed to a lamppost, trying to fight off a 6'3" member of the group as he attempted to shave my eyebrows off. Fortunately, I succeeded or more realistically he just gave up. Thank you Andy and thank you Matt and Ivan for all of your help stopping him. Oh no, my mistake there wasn't any. I still have the photo of you both laughing.

Matt and I go back to 1990 in uniform at Braunstone Police Station and he ended up as my boss in Major Crime in 2012. Wherever we have worked it has gone well for us and less well for those we have investigated. He started coming on the trips in 2013 but more on him later.

Back to the Blackpool golf trip in 2008. On the first night we had a reasonable time but there was definitely a *feet sticking to the carpets* sensation in some pubs. I wasn't feeling 100% and around midnight I thought it would be a good idea to go back to the hotel and get some shut-eye ready for a long day on the course. I spoke to Lee and he told me he felt the same, so leaving the hardcore drinking we got a taxi back to Heron's Reach.

We walked into the hotel reception to get our keys and waited behind a chap checking in. He looked familiar. Then we realised. It was Roy Chubby Brown or Royston Vasey as The League of Gentlemen had revealed him to really be called.

I remembered reading that despite his exceptionally profane stage persona, he is in real life, a guy who doesn't like the effing and jeffing at all.

I approached him and asked him very politely if I could take a photo of him with my mate.

'Of course you fucking can son', he replied and we got a nice shot of him with Lee.

He said, *'You lads are very polite. Some cunts just come up and take one. They get told to fuck right off!'*

We asked him what he was in town for.

'I'm here to do a show in this fuckin shit hole', he said. *'I'm on the bastard pier tomorrow night. What a fucking hole. I'll be surprised if the fuckin' thing doesn't fall in the bastard sea.'*

Just goes to show, don't believe everything you read.

Some of the boys found him still in the bar when they got back and had a beer and a laugh with him. They reported much the same thing. Funny on stage, funny off it.

Thomo was back for his second year and I drew his name out in Eddie's sweep. I was feeling lucky as I knew I had already won £49 on the Bonus Ball draw. That feeling changed when I walked outside after the morning team event, with my lunch and a pint of Diet Coke, to find Thomo finishing off a pint of beer. Then he got up and fetched another one.

'Thomo!' I shouted. *'You're my horse this afternoon. Get off that stuff and get some coffee down you. You're out with Blackie and Alan. They'll rip you to shreds.'*

He just grinned at me and out came the Frank Bruno laugh, *'Hurgh hurgh. Don't worry about me Shutts, I won't let you down.'*

In the event it was the closest ever competition. I collected the cards in and saw that I had three people all on thirty-four points. The boys had found it tough. Thomo was one of the three but so was the defending champ PD. Darren made up the trio. Using the usual countback method, I smiled to myself when I saw the result. Thomo had done it, PD was second. It got a massive cheer when I announced it at the presentation.

Thomo is a popular guy but the real laugh was that Alan and Blackie, the masters at talking anyone, especially each other out of the game, had been done up like kippers by a bloke who didn't even mean to. Thomo was invited to speak as he took the trophy and had the green jacket placed on his shoulders by PD.

'Laurel and Hardy here spent the entire game psyching each other out of every putt and then on the seventeenth they suddenly realised I was beating the pair of them and they both started on me. I told them, boys you have no chance of getting inside my head. Even I don't know what the hell is going on in there. Hurgh hurgh!'

Scouse won the King Rabbit title, awarded every year for the best twenty-four plus handicapper. I haven't kept full records of that award over the years but I remember this one because he blew up on about the seventeenth and threatened to walk off because he thought he was playing so badly.

Then the person marking his card told him he was probably on course to win the Rabbits prize, so he stayed on and actually scored a couple more points to seal it. He called it a day though after Blackpool and I'm not sure if he still plays or not.

From memory, I was on the winning Texas Scramble team which meant M&S vouchers, I took the Bonus Ball £49 and scooped another £30 on my horse Thomo, so it was my most successful trip ever, financially. Well, apart from the previous year when the boys gave me a tenth anniversary wad of cash to pay for my trip in full. Much appreciated gents.

Meanwhile the Major chuntered all the way home after coming fourth and out of the prizes for the *third* consecutive year. Gordon equalled his best ever score of seven points to give him a total of seventeen over the previous three years. It had looked up for him when he found himself on six points after three holes but the next time he troubled the scoreboard was with a point on the eighteenth.

Professionally I had moved on again and after a spell as an acting uniformed inspector I took a job aimed at getting me promoted; staff officer to the Assistant Chief Constable before getting a post as Temporary DI at Loughborough Police Station.

Personally, the first half of the year was shit because my Dad died suddenly in the April. He didn't even get to see my boy's first birthday on our planned trip to Jersey, which was really sad for us all. I miss him to this day and wish we could go for just one more pint.

Chepstow 2009

TIME FOR a trip back across the border. Alan, The Power and I all availed ourselves of the Major's offer to drive in his Ford S-Max or '*The European Car of the Year 2007*'. Not that he banged on about that or tried to overcharge us for fuel. Much.

Alan cooked us a breakfast before we set off and The Power paid the toll on the way over the bridge into Wales. I said I would get it on the way back knowing full well that you only paid on the West bound side.

I picked Chepstow because it looked like a cracking course with a Marriott Hotel to stay in and we wanted to go to the races. That turned into a good night with quite a few of us coming out well ahead. The Marriott did me proud too. Instead of being given a standard room like everyone else, I got a little one bedroom cottage in a row of about half a dozen of them, on a green near the entrance.

As soon as we arrived at Chepstow Racecourse, I saw my next door neighbour from home, a racecourse bookie, all set up and trading. He told me to let the boys know that for us he would match the best price any of the others had going so he got a fair bit of business out of us. I managed to wheedle one decent tip from him which I put plenty on with a different bookie and it placed, as he had forecast, so that paid for my night out. I've never had one from him since by the way!

The next day the golf went well although I buggered up the handicaps with a couple of people. The first one was Andy, a non-police mate of Jason's who came on his first trip of several. Just when

Jason was playing badly enough for PD to have no complaints, up pops his mate with about twenty-two points from the front nine. I bumped into PD part way round and he left me in no doubt of what he thought of Andy's twenty-one handicap.

As it turned out, Andy then fell apart and ended up only getting another ten points to finish joint fourth with Baras on thirty-two points.

Lee and Alan both played well for thirty-five points but were left trailing in the wake of the winner who ripped the course up with forty-two points. Playing off a handicap of twenty-eight, Eddie played to about twenty-one or twenty-two. And this time PD was as culpable as me.

Eddie, a man of genuine integrity, approached me before we played and told me he had been playing a lot and playing well. He said it would be unfair for him to play off twenty-eight, the same as the likes of me, Jon and The Power, who all played about four times a year.

I was really doubtful, especially after seeing him tee off in the Texas Scramble like he was playing with a broom. I knew that he and PD had played a different course the day before, so I asked PD what he thought. PD knows his golf and I trusted his opinion. I told him that Eddie wanted to play off twenty-four, just high enough to keep him in the Rabbits competition.

PD laughed. He said, '*Simon he was absolute garbage yesterday. He knocked it round in about 110. He is a twenty-eight handicapper all day long.*' And so it was.

Never did we have a more popular champion. He was thrilled to bits with it. He even phoned his elderly, Leeds United supporting Mum, who I had met a few times and he put me on the phone to her. I was the only person allowed to call him Eddie whilst talking to her. His real name is John and she insisted on that from everyone else he worked with or she wouldn't speak to them. She was really happy for him too, even though, as she put it, '*he's still a flipping Leicester fan*'. The lovely 'Mrs M', as I called her, sadly passed away in April 2021.

Eddie's win made my day and after a few beers we decided to celebrate properly by having a go at the karaoke in a Chepstow bar. Note to self: *Don't do 'Three Lions' in a Welsh karaoke bar. They don't like it.* We escaped unscathed, mainly because a couple of the local hobbledehoys who expressed their displeasure had a little look at Phil, an old friend who you would have to be mentally unstable to want to fight and they thought better of it. I did try and punch him once actually. That fight lasted less than a second, never involved him using his hands at all and ended up with him picking me up off the police station residents block kitchen floor and telling me to behave.

Anyway, back at the Marriott hotel, Eddie, The Major and I sat outside in the still warm late evening, on the lawn in front of my cottage. We drank Scotch Whisky and Irish Whiskey into the wee small hours, arguing about when to use ice and having one of the most pleasant nights I can ever remember on a trip.

Evington Place, Leicester where Russell was shot in the leg by someone we thought we knew but could never positively identify.

The 8th at Meyrick Park, a tricky par 3. I rarely troubled the green.

With Greg in Bournemouth. He was a popular winner in Reading in 2011. I played reasonably well with a bad back, prompting some to unkindly suggest I should turn up injured every year.

The takeaway on Linton Street in Leicester where in 2012 the popular owner and family man, Dogan Dogan was savagely robbed and murdered.

Bournemouth 2010

BACK TO Bournemouth was the popular choice when I asked around. It was not a memorable trip for any golfing reason. Jason's mate Andy came again and having frightened me with his front nine in Chepstow, I cut him to eighteen. This time he played even better than before and didn't crack up halfway round. He made a mockery of his handicap and got to forty-four points, the highest ever winning score.

The person I felt most sorry for was Baras, who played a blinder off his genuine handicap and got thirty-seven points only to come second. I willed my old Class 7/87 pal to nick it but through no fault of his own he came up way short.

At night, once again we found ourselves in Spearmint Rhino, where I had taken to standing with Eddie and the Major, just to stay out of the way of ladies asking if we wanted private dances. Also, because Eddie had somehow managed to do a deal with one of the barmen in which we got an extension to the happy hour £1 a bottle deal.

We had been in there a while and had just realised that the beer had gone back up to its normal silly price, which signalled time to go. Out of the blue, a chap came up to me and asked me if I was *'in charge of this lot'*.

Alarm bells. Bells that didn't particularly switch off when he told me he was the head doorman.

'I'm not in charge of them,' I said. *'We're on a golf trip and I'm the organiser. Why?'*

'I'll tell you fucking why' he said, aggressively. *'One of your bloody mates wanted a private dance and tried to pay on his credit card on this.'*

He held up a credit card machine.

'His card was refused and when we told him he ripped it out and ran off and the machine is shagged now.'

I assured him that he had got the wrong group of lads.

Whilst I can't say that none of our trippers ever had a little fun with a dance, I knew for sure that none of the regulars you have been reading about did this sort of thing. Most of us knew each other's wives for a start and everyone also knew the Blabber Mouth Kev story from Bath, so even those who might have been tempted, despite this and the effect it could have on a police career, did *not* go there.

Another reason, apparently, was how much it cost. I went to the toilet at one point and as I was there in walked Bingo, a first timer who was finding his feet for a few years before winning three titles on the trot. I can't remember the name of the character played by Brian Glover in Porridge but talking to Bingo was a bit like talking to that guy.

'Ay up Shutts this is a right place. I don't know where to look. One of them gels has just come up to me and asked me if I wanted a private dance. Then she gave me a price,' he said.

'What did you say?' I asked.

'I told her, no way love, I could get a Sky Sports subscription for less than that.'

Back in the moment and the doorman was still standing there. And now, seemingly out of nowhere, he was holding up a credit card.

'He left this behind.' I looked at the card and sighed. Eric.

Eric was a lad who came on a few trips and for some reason had ended up rooming with me this year. Fortunately, the card machine sprang back into life and the doorman gave me the card back, as well as some advice for Eric. It was along the lines of *'if he comes back in here it won't be fuckin' pretty.'* I *was* listening to him but privately I was just feeling relieved that nobody had told him we were police officers.

Then he said, *'By the way I know you're all coppers.'*

Eric was nowhere to be seen, not in the club or any of the pubs we went to afterwards. When I got back to the room about 2.30am he was in his bed, pretending to be asleep.

Needless to say, a few people mentioned it at breakfast.

Reading 2011

READING WAS one of my least popular choices. The course and the hotel were nice though and I went back to sharing with the Major. Eric could look after himself.

As it was I had an horrendous back injury, something that has plagued me for years and the Major ended up carrying my holdall as well as his own and his clubs, moaning every step of the way and making up stuff about what was really wrong with me.

We stayed in the hotel at first and after a while we saw a few familiar faces. There was a group of football managers on some kind of coaching course. We saw Gianfranco Zola, Mick McCarthy, who was then the Wolves manager and Chris Kiwomya, all round a table chatting.

Baras's brother was a professional footballer and is now a well-known manager and he had met Kiwomya before, so he went and had a chat with him. Then when he came back, he said he had got an idea. When I had left Major Crime to get promoted Baras had stayed and he was still a DS there at this time.

The unit had just evolved into an arm of a new regional homicide team as part of the East Midlands Special Operations Unit or EMSOU for short. The boss, a Chief Superintendent, was called Andy Hough. And he was a Wolves fan.

'I'm going to get McCarthy's autograph for the new boss!' said Baras.

No amount of calling him a brown noser or an arse licker could dissuade him. He grabbed a card from somewhere and scribbled on it.

'There you go' he said. *'I've written to Andy Hough, best wishes, so all Big Mick has to do is sign his name. I'm sure he won't mind.'* I looked at the card.

'Baras you've spelt his name wrong' I said. *'It's H-O-U-G-H not H-O-F-F you muppet.'*

'Is it?' he said. And he scribbled out Hoff and wrote Hough just above.

A minute later Mick McCarthy was walking towards us and Baras spoke to him.

'Excuse me Mr McCarthy' he said. The big man stopped in the middle of us and looked us up and down. We had had a few.

'All right lads' he drawled.

Baras presented him with the card and asked for the autograph. He glanced at it, raised an eyebrow, shrugged and signed it. The he walked off smiling and shaking his head.

The golf was a quiet affair with little in the way of controversy. PD was back after missing the previous year but he was restricted to second place. Greg, the Scottish dog handler finally got the win that his golfing talent deserved.

I finished eleventh, prompting some unkind people to point out that I ought to turn up every year with a bad back. Whether I did or didn't, we wouldn't be coming back to Reading. Despite the hotel being one of the better ones, the town was as dull as its reputation and it was a half hour ride in a taxi away to boot.

Back at work, I got involved in one of the more bizarre investigations of my career. It was one that when it finally came to trial and the offender was sentenced, His Honour Judge Pert, would describe the events that had unfolded as *'the stuff of movies'*.

That summer, I had been overlooked for a return to the Major Crime team for the second time in three years. I'll explain my thoughts on that in the next chapter. What *did* happen was I was told I would be moving back to the city in a sideways Detective Inspector move.

Then one Saturday morning in September, I was the on-call DI for Leicestershire when about 7am I got a call from the Power, who was by now a DS and was on the Night Crime Car. This car provides the sole detective cover for the million residents of Leicester, Leicestershire and Rutland between about eleven and seven each night. The crew are usually a DS and a DC and they offer advice and deal with any serious crime that comes in during those hours.

The Power and his crew mate had been dealing with a situation all night after a ninety-one year old lady had been found in a distressed state outside her home in Hinckley. Getting any solid information from her was difficult but they had worked out that someone had come into her bedroom, in the bungalow she lived in and woken her up. It looked like she had been sexually assaulted.

I took the job on as SIO and got the specialist staff from the force's rape investigation unit, *Signa*l, to work on it with me. My DS was a guy called Mark who had been at Loughborough when I was there. Six years later he would succeed me as an SIO in Major Crime when I retired. The DC who became the OIC was Kate. They were both outstanding. I had not worked directly with the Signal team before and they all really impressed me.

We took a day or so to work out who had done it and initially we were looking at a sex offender who was in the wrong place at the wrong time. The pieces didn't quite fit for him though and then we got some information from the Probation Service about a seventeen year old youth called Lawrence who had slipped a tag he had been wearing. He was supposed to have been staying at a particular address and he was on a curfew but as this deadline approached he was drunk, had apparently been using drugs and was getting extremely aggressive.

His probation officer was called and she did her best to calm him down but it was probably a job beyond the best of negotiators. He legged it and at that point she should have reported the breach of the tag but she did not. The next day he carried out a robbery on a young lad riding his bike in the town and the lad knew his name and quickly reported it. It was all a day too late for our victim. Let's be clear though, the probation officer could never have known that and the chances of the Hinckley Police having the resources to go looking for him if she had reported it, are minimal.

We pieced together Lawrence's movements and established that he had been to the victim's home with two mates late on the Saturday night. He had gone in to see what he could steal to sell for more booze and drugs. The other two waited outside and did not know what happened inside.

What the victim told the specialist officers who interviewed her on video on the Sunday was that she had woken to find Lawrence in her room and when she challenged him he got on top of her and covered her face with a pillow. He then sexually assaulted her and tried to rape her; she said she felt his penis on her leg. Then, having not committed the rape, he left the victim where she was, passed a TV and some jewellery out to the others and they all left.

Lawrence and the other two were arrested and taken to Beaumont Leys Police Station. We quickly realised that there was something different about this character. Something dangerous. He was only seventeen but he was over six feet tall and he was very athletically built. He was very engaging with the interviewers and they were uncomfortable with the way he was constantly looking at his surroundings, checking doors and gates, looking at people coming and going in the custody suite. I told them and I told the custody staff that I wanted him searched before and after every movement of him, whether that was to and from interview or to see a solicitor or a doctor or whatever. He stole a pen after one interview and had taken the casing off it before he was found with it. God knows what he was going to do with it.

He initially denied that he gone into the bungalow at all but when he realised that his two co-accused had turned on him and told us what had happened, he accepted that part. He only got really upset when the direct accusations of sexual assault were covered. He became quite aggressive and seemed embarrassed by it all. He denied it totally.

He was charged with the robbery on the lad in Hinckley, burglary, sexual assault and attempted rape. In court he was remanded into custody and sent to a young offenders' prison in Wetherby in West Yorkshire. Then the fun and games began.

Lawrence immediately began to plan his escape. This part of his story is perhaps more fascinating to me than others. A passion of mine is World War Two history and a subject I am fairly well read on is prisoners of war and escaping. Katy even took me to Colditz Castle in Germany as a fortieth birthday present. I had read the Colditz Story by Pat Reid when I was twelve and was immediately hooked. The next day, in the absence of another one on the same subject, I started it again. And yes, I do still have Escape from Colditz the board game!

Anyway, over a period of a few days of going to the gym in a supervised group of twenty or thirty inmates, Lawrence tore pieces of material from a climbing wall, took it back with him and gradually matted it into a homemade rope. Then he stole a pair of weightlifting gloves. On the route between his accommodation and the gym he worked out a blind spot into which he could duck whilst the group walked back from the gym after an evening session.

On the selected day he did just this and it worked. He knew he had a limited amount of time because the prisoners were counted on departure to the gym and counted again when they got back to the accommodation block. As soon as the group were out of sight, he raced around the building to a tall fence topped with razor wire and slung the rope over the top. He pulled it wearing the gloves and was happy it had snagged at the top but as soon as he started to climb up, it snapped and he fell onto his back.

He thought that would be that and he waited for the alarm to sound and the guards to come running. But no-one came. Unbeknown to him, the two guards supervising the gym visit had done the count and then argued about the number. They decided that they must have counted incorrectly on the way out as none of the prisoners could have gone anywhere. Doh! Had either of them read *The One That Got Away*, about Franz von Werra, the only German to fully escape from the allies during the war, they might at least have had a look!

Anyway, Lawrence realised he had another chance so he climbed up a lamppost and jumped onto a wall standing next to it. The wall was actually a similar height to the fence but whilst it ran straight *towards* the fence, it stopped short with a huge gap in between. Undeterred, Lawrence sprinted along the wall and took off like Greg Rutherford, landing right in the razor wire. He was cut to pieces but got down the other side and he was out.

The first thing he did was look for a lift and he found one with a truck driver in a service area. He knew that his absence would soon be discovered by prison officers with a bit more about them and the alarm would be sounded. He wanted to be out of the area quickly. The lorry was travelling North East and when they reached Stockton-on-Tees he got out. He then broke into a house and stole car keys and a car. It was a pink Nissan Micra with a yellow picture of the cartoon character, Tweety Pie, on the bonnet. He drove that straight back to Leicestershire.

The next day the balloon went up when Lawrence was spotted in the village of Earl Shilton, just outside Hinckley in Leicestershire. A massive search operation was commenced and we realised he had gone into hiding somewhere in gardens. He was found by a police officer, sitting in a conservatory, watching TV. He had black aerosol paint all over his trainers. He later told interviewers he had been in a shed when he heard a police dog bark so he used the paint to put them off the scent. He said he had also spread himself out into a star shape to minimise his heat signal to the police helicopter. I have no idea whether either of these things worked but I was certainly learning more about this unusual and dangerous young man.

We had him back at Beaumont and dealt with him for the new offences. We charged him with escaping, burglary in Stockton, theft of petrol on the way south and criminal damage to a shed he had broken into. I decided we would not use the contracted force security company to take him to court. I was not trusting this highly intelligent escaper to anyone else unless I had to.

I picked the van crew to transport him and got two extra staff in the back. I briefed them on Lawrence and also personally sat in the back, with him in the little caged area next to me. He knew I was in charge of the investigation and he was happy to chat to me. For the whole of the journey to court he was looking around, checking out the door seals and the locks on the van and watching the officers. The docks at Leicester Magistrates Court are all secure from top to bottom so there was no chance of him doing a Russell and jumping out of one. Once remanded he was sent to Hindley, near Wigan, a more secure young offenders' prison.

A couple of weeks later, in mid-October, I went to Tenerife for a much anticipated week in the hot autumn sunshine with a group of family and friends. We got back late one night and I was awoken early the next morning by a ringing phone. He had escaped again a couple of days earlier. I headed off to a briefing for the operation to catch him again and I arrived to find that they had placed a DI called Chris in charge of it and they hadn't realised I was back from leave. I made it quite clear that was not going to continue. Chris was busy enough with his own workload and only too happy to pack his stuff up and let me have it back.

Over the course of that afternoon and the next day we set about finding him. I was absolutely certain that even if he didn't come back to Hinckley again, he would contact someone nearby who would know where he was. And so it proved.

After a tip off the next afternoon, I sent an excellent detective called Jo, who had worked for me in Loughborough, to see a girl who we thought might know something. Many people would have got nothing but Jo did what she was good at. She took her time and talked to the girl. After what seemed like ages she called me and gave me an address in Birmingham. Apparently it was the home of Lawrence's half-sister. I sent a team there and he was a found hiding under a bed.

And he had an even more outrageous tale to tell this time.

Once at Hindley he had cased the place looking for an opportunity and he found one in the shower block, where there were bars that he thought he could squeeze through in front of the windows. He did this and kicked the glass out of the windows. Outside he found himself on a high wall. He jumped down and then climbed up and over a razor wired outer fence, cutting his hands again in the process. Then he stole a pedal cycle and got out of the area as quickly as he could.

By the time he got to a residential area, it was mid-evening. He wanted to break into a house to steal car keys again to get properly away. It was a bit early for people to be in bed but he garden-hopped, trying a few back doors, leaving blood on several of them until he finally found one open. He quietly went in and found himself in a kitchen. He squinted through a door and could see an elderly couple watching TV. He couldn't see any car keys but he managed to steal a jacket and a mobile phone.

Once outside again he tried to work out where he was and in doing this he approached a group of girls and lads about his own age. He actually told them that he was an escaper and they laughed and encouraged him but when he told them where he had got the jacket and phone from, one of was less amused. It was his grandparents' house he said. Unfazed, Lawrence said sorry, gave him the coat and phone and moved on.

At one point he broke into a property that was empty with a 'to let' sign at the front. He found that the central heating worked so he ran a bath and dried himself on curtains. He slept there for two nights, using the curtains as a bed cover too. He went out late on the second night and broke into a closed Chinese takeaway where he stole prawn crackers, alcohol and cash.

The next morning, he found a bus to Manchester Rail Station where, unable to see any trains going to Leicester, he caught one to Birmingham and persuaded his half-sister to put him up. He carried on committing crime in Birmingham, including burglary and theft from a car before he was arrested.

We dealt with him for everything again. If there was any thought that his stories were fanciful, these were soon dispelled. The houses with blood on the back door handles were found and visited, as was the Chinese takeaway. He was charged with escaping again, as well as burglary and the other offences and once more I insisted we would be taking him to court. The van was parked in the yard at Beaumont Leys and he had been loaded up into the cage at the back by the time I climbed into the middle section and sat down next to him on other side of the mesh. He looked at me and grinned.

'Hello Boss. The custody sergeant said you were in Spain,' he said.

'I was,' I replied, *'but I came back to catch you.'*

'Oh well' he said, *'Next time I get out I'm going to Spain in the back of an HGV so you can have another holiday catching me again.'*

Kate and Mark then did the hard work that follows charges and took the case forward, preparing it for trial. It wasn't as complex as a murder and there wasn't a lot for me to do until we began to prep for trial. My concern then was security. I was sure that if Lawrence gave evidence, the judge would not agree to any request for him to be handcuffed. It would, maybe quite rightly, be considered too prejudicial to let the jury see that.

The first thing I did was get in touch with the prison Lawrence had now been taken to. No more Young Offenders Institution (YOI). He was now eighteen and although that's still an age in which you can go to a YOI, he had been sent to an adult jail in the home counties. The staff were immediately on my wavelength and we reached an agreement that five of them would travel to court with him each day and they would take primacy in the guarding of him in court. It would not be left to the court security staff.

I wasn't allowed to meet with the trial judge, a man called Pert, prior to trial so to discuss security I met with Judge Hammond, who in 2004 had been the judge to sentence Russell for his leap from the dock. He let me have a wander about the corridors behind the courtrooms and I concluded that if Lawrence got that far he would probably go for a jump from one of the first floor windows there. Judge Hammond agreed that I could place an officer in the space behind the door through which Judge Pert would enter the court. He also agreed that I could have two officers in court, in uniform, with full PPE, that is to say batons and Captor Spray, nasty stuff that messes your eyes up. I told him that Mark, Kate and I would also be in court. Lawrence would be in the secure dock and if he came out to give evidence the five prison officers plus the three of us would be around him like a slip field.

On the first day of trial, he never left the dock so there were no issues. Judge Pert had been quick to spot the uniformed officers at the back of the court. He would have been told about them by Hammond. He couldn't resist a quip before the jury came in.

He said, '*If Mr Lawrence tries to get away, I would suggest that the two uniformed officers sitting right back there will be no more use than ornament.*' We all laughed politely at his little joke.

Pert was a judge who often made us laugh. One day, at Christmas time, I was in court waiting for a particular case to come up while Pert was hearing an application for a man accused of a serious offence to be released on bail, pending trial. The barrister making the application was a man, now a judge himself actually, who rumour had it Pert hated for a personal reason I'm not commenting on here. Rumour also had it that the barrister, whom we shall call Mr Smith, hated him back. Both had a reputation for being pretty aggressive when poked.

Mr Smith prefaced his application with an odd request of Pert.

He said, '*Should your honour not find in my favour today, would it be possible for me to return tomorrow to try again?*'

'*I'm not following you Mr Smith*' said Pert. '*If I refuse your client bail today are you asking me if you can have another go at convincing me some other time?*'

'*I'm just asking your honour for a little latitude in that should you not favour my application today, you might let me return and try again.*' It was an odd request.

Pert took a sip of the San Pellegrino sparkling water that was a permanent fixture on his bench and looked over the top of his spectacles.

'*Mr Smith*' he growled. '*It might be Christmas, but I'm not Santa.*' Bail was quickly refused.

Back in the Lawrence trial, the first day went off with no drama. The prison officers were an efficient crew of five headed by an old sweat who looked like he had seen it all before. They looked alert and like they knew their jobs, which reassured me.

The next morning the same crew appeared and I asked the senior man if there had been any problems. There had. One the way home, with Lawrence in one of the jail cubicles on the prison truck, the smoke alarm suddenly went off. They were southbound on the M1 so they had to pull over onto the hard shoulder. Lawrence had somehow got hold of a match and a cigarette and had lit up in his cubicle.

'*He was testing us*' said the officer. '*He wanted to see if the security was like it is at those two places he has escaped from. He was discouraged.*' I didn't ask what that meant but the officer went on '*This morning we went to get him from his cell and he just said oh fucking hell not you lot again.*'

I thought Lawrence looked a bit thinner and less defiant than when I had last seen him during the investigation but I had no doubt he was still a threat. Eventually the day came around when he was due to give evidence. Pert had, as predicted, refused to sanction him being cuffed as he did that, so he would be able to walk freely from the dock to the witness box in open court.

I was still not happy that we had it covered so I made a call to the Force Operations Inspector and he dispatched two more officers to me. One I used in the body of the court, to supplement the slip field which included me, Kate, Mark and the prison officers. The other was an acting sergeant called Sam. He was a tall and athletic looking lad I didn't know but he looked capable. I told him he would be positioned out of sight of the court, behind the door that the judge entered by. This was the obvious escape route for Lawrence if he got past the rest of us. I told Sam what I wanted if Lawrence kicked off. I showed him his position behind the judge's bench. He had a view through a spyhole in the door.

'If we are fighting with him I do not want you coming in and helping unless the judge is in danger,' I said. *'You are here in case he gets past us. If you see him coming this way be prepared and if he comes through this door you put him down with your baton, no dicking about. You OK with that?'* He was.

As it turned out we had no problems. Lawrence perhaps didn't fancy his chances, I don't know. Our barrister, Felicity, took him apart when he gave evidence and the judge's summing up didn't do him any favours either. He was found guilty and sentenced to an IPP, a scheme since abolished. It stands for Imprisonment for Public Protection and was designed to make sure offenders who were a danger to the public but did not qualify for a life sentence were controlled, particularly around the conditions of their release. All IPPs really did though was confuse people, especially victims and their families. Lawrence was told he must serve at least four years but the Attorney General, Dominic Grieve QC appealed it on the grounds that it was unduly lenient and it was later increased to six years.

I have always thought it was a real example of a life wasted. We had heard that as a child Lawrence was beaten, sometimes with a weapon. A bike chain was mentioned. It was a sad story and he had clearly been through proper trauma. Who knows what a success he could have been, maybe in the services, if someone had cared about him and shown him some love?

Bottom line for me though was his poor victim. She never lived in her home again and she died having never recovered from the events of that horrendous night. That is on Lawrence.

Bournemouth 2012

I NEVER got round to mentioning it but I had consolidated my temporary Detective Inspector position at Loughborough by achieving substantive promotion, in post, in the autumn of 2008.

Now, after three years and eight months as an area DI, I got what I wanted. A job in EMSOU-Major Crime. I had been prevented from joining before, largely due to a clash with a very senior detective officer who I won't bother to name.

He used to say that you were either in the box or out of it. The box was the *Shit Box* and if you were in it you were in the shit with him and your chances of progression as a detective were limited. He was a very bright guy and he had ideas and drive that I feel I have to give him the credit for. He just spoiled it with his draconian attitude and claims that he was some kind of old school veteran detective, when in fact he had joined the force a couple of years after I did.

I had made the mistake of failing to invite him to open a training day I had organised for the entire Leicestershire CID and so I was '*in the box*'.

Baras knew him better than me and bumped into him in the canteen on the way to this event. Baras asked him if he was coming to open it. He said no he had not been invited and that I, having got out of the box briefly, was back in it permanently.

Unfortunately, sometimes I can't help myself. I had already had a phone conversation with this man after I realised what I had done and tried to put the error - the let's face it *very bloody small error* –

right. He chucked his toys out of the pram and refused to attend. He then tried to berate me and I had to stop him and tell him that I was a forty-five year old bloke and I wasn't going to jump into the corner and start crying.

Then I catch him out slagging me off to my oldest mate in the job. I was not going to let that pass me by unanswered. I texted him and asked what box he meant – *was it the shit box*? He didn't much like that but I didn't much care.

Happily for me, by the autumn of 2011, Matt and Alan were the DCIs in Major Crime and when they were asked who they wanted from a shortlist of about four, they both picked me and in January 2012 I started.

Six days into what was to be my last ever posting in the force, the next career defining job in my life came in. Alan had said that one of the reasons I was picked was because, with my experience of major enquiries, I would be able to '*hit the ground running*'. Operation Terry, the investigation into the murder of a man called Dogan Dogan, certainly put that to the test.

On Sunday 8th January 2012, my new team of two Detective Sergeants and five DCs were on call and on duty at Beaumont Leys Police Station in Leicester. About 2pm I was just deciding to let them off early for a couple of hours when I took a call from the experienced on-call DCI, Tom from Northamptonshire.

'*We've got a murder*,' he told me. '*I'll come to you and we'll work out what we are going to do.*'

A few hours later, togged up in white suits, Tom and I, along with a Home Office Forensic Pathologist and Barbara, in my opinion the best and most experienced of the region's senior crime scene investigators (CSI), entered the bedsit bedroom of Dogan Dogan, the Turkish owner of the Aladdin pizza takeaway below where we now stood. Dogan was dead and lay before us in his trashed bedroom.

Over the next day or so we established that Dogan owned two takeaways, Aladdin in Leicester and Pizzaman in Lutterworth, fourteen miles to the south of the city. His home was in North London and he would habitually live three or four days out of his bedsit above Aladdin and three or four days in London.

We learned that on the night of Saturday 7th January he had spent the evening working in Lutterworth. His manager in Leicester had put most of the takings from the Leicester branch in an envelope under the door to Dogan's room at midnight. Around 1.30am the last two staff members to leave left the remaining couple of hundred pounds in the till for him to pick up later, when he returned with the Lutterworth takings.

We saw him leave Lutterworth, courtesy of a clear CCTV image, around 2am. He was back in Leicester less than thirty minutes later. A camera opposite Aladdin picked up a reflection in a window of him parking and entering the shop where I dare say he took the money from the till upstairs to his room. The hazard lights on his car flashed to indicate he was locking it.

To get to his room Dogan had to go outside into the rear yard for the premises and walk up a set of wooden steps to the door. Inside was a long narrow corridor with three rooms on the right and nothing on the left. The rooms were a bathroom, a kitchen and a storage room with chest freezers full of burgers and pizzas, as well as shelves stacked up with pizza boxes and takeaway cartons.

At the far end, which you could see from the entrance, the corridor zig zagged and then in front of the next bit of floor was the door to Dogan's bedsit. There was another flat upstairs but this was empty and unused.

An hour after Dogan had returned, the lights on his car could be seen to flash again. Dogan was probably dead by then. His body was discovered when his shop manager came to open up for the Sunday trade around 2pm the next afternoon. He was hog tied with a yellow rope going from around his neck to around his wrists behind his back. He was then wrapped in four layers of material including his own sweatshirt, a towel and a bed sheet which was tied in a very intricate knot.

He was wearing grey tracksuit bottoms but his feet were bare; in fact, one foot was trapped underneath an empty draw that appeared to have been pulled from a chest of drawers in the bedsit. His legs were tied tightly in the same yellow twine; so tightly in fact that it left deep indentations in his calves. Trapped in this part of rope was the finger section from a latex glove.

I mentioned at the start of my story that investigating murder and bringing people to justice is the greatest responsibility a detective has. I met Dogan's wife and family on several occasions. They were lovely people. Once, when I arrived with the Family Liaison Officer Kev, to see them at their home in London, we could see that something new had upset them.

Dogan's youngest daughter was about eight at the time and they explained that she kept going off and sitting in her Dad's wardrobe, just to be able to smell his clothes, maybe hoping he would turn up in the week to wear them. It was heart-breaking and we didn't have any worthwhile advice to give them. All we could offer was that we would get the bastards who had done this. Even now it makes me shudder to think about it.

Our investigation was thorough and as Tom's number two I was allowed a certain amount of latitude to direct things because he was unavoidably busy trying to sort out an extremely high profile job in Northants. The previous year, on the day of the royal wedding of William and Kate, all four members of the Ding family had been slaughtered by a man called Anxiang Du over a petty grudge he held. Tom had done a great job with it. He was a very thorough SIO and he knew who was responsible but Du had fled the country and was being a bugger to find.

We did everything properly on the Dogan Dogan job and chased down every line of enquiry but in that key twenty four to forty eight hour period we got nowhere fast. Forensically the scene in the flat looked like our best bet to make progress and our crime scene investigators Barbara and Ken (yes really) took their time and harvested it for evidence.

We had established that Dogan's mobile phone and wallet had been taken as well as the car keys and shop keys. We thought that the flashing hazard lights on his car around 3.30am was the offenders with the car keys but they left the car there and didn't take the six or seven pounds in coins that was inside. We estimated that they had gotten away with about £3,000 in takings from Aladdin and Pizzaman.

One of the better things I gave time to, as it turned out, was a press release. I gave out Dogan's full details and put out an appeal out for information. Four days later a man called in from a street next to Leicester Racecourse, two miles from Aladdin. He had found a pile of rubbish dumped outside his garden wall. He said it had been there for a few days but on Thursday 12th January he finally got around to clearing it up.

When he did so he found himself looking at an odd collection of bits of latex glove, a sock and some broken keys. One of the keys had a keyring attached with the word *Dogan* clearly printed on it. The man remembered reading about Dogan's murder in the Leicester Mercury two days earlier, so he called the police.

Around the same time, we had our first forensic breakthrough. The piece of latex glove that had been trapped in the bindings around Dogan's legs had yielded a DNA profile of an illegal overstayer in the country from Afghanistan; one Wali Khan.

That was the good news. The bad news was nobody knew where he was. He had entered the country the previous year in the back of a truck and had been detained. He had applied for asylum and been given a temporary release while his application was considered. He failed to turn up for the result of this, which was to return him to the country he had just come from, France I think.

A few weeks later he was stopped by a Met officer and arrested again. He was taken to a detention centre but then allowed to go out if he *promised* to hand himself in to get on the plane. You must promise Wali. Scout's honour. Pinkie promise. Cross your heart and hope to die. I can only assume he had his fingers crossed.

Some good intelligence work led us to a report of a middle eastern looking male called Wali making regular visits to see a sixteen year old girl in a children's home in Leicester. The staff were visited and they said that this man Wali was always driven to the home in a VW Passat by another man who may have been Indian or Pakistani. They gave the registration number but somewhere along the way a digit was mistaken and more work was needed to work out what the real number of the Passat was.

The sixteen year old girl was seen and she filled in some of the blanks. She said his name was Wali Khan, he was from Afghanistan and she loved him. She didn't know his mate's name but she did know something had gone wrong for them and his mate had not been able to bring him to the home for a while because he had sold his car.

Cutting a long story short we ended up with an address in Leicester for Wali Khan, about ten days after the murder. Surveillance officers waited for him to emerge from it and then followed him, with another man of possibly Indian or Pakistani origin, to a little Fiat Punto.

I was in the surveillance control room with Brett – one of the golf trip boys who had been insulted by grumpy Trevor in Aberystwyth. When it started to get a little dusky, I was worried we might lose them, so I asked Brett to get his team to strike and arrest both men. They did this, calling forward a marked car whose officers dragged the pair of them out.

Lying on the front passenger seat was Dogan Dogan's mobile phone. Jackpot.

Wali Khan and the Pakistani man, Naveed Naveed (another double name just to complicate things) were interviewed and denied everything. They would probably have been better served making no comment to all questions but in the event they told lie after provable lie.

Naveed, we realised eventually, was paranoid about being caught out forensically. He reeled off the most bizarre story. He said that he *had* been to the premises on the night of the murder but this was not at the time we were asking him about, this was several hours earlier, around 10pm. He said he had been looking for a flat for his girlfriend to rent and this one had been advertised. He couldn't remember where.

He said the door at the top of steps had been left open for him so he let himself in. According to him he went to the loo, washed his hands, went in the kitchen, looked in the freezers, had a glass of water, went in the bedsit, sat on the bed, opened a window, switched the telly on, probably touched all the furniture and then left. I remember saying to his interviewers, why don't you ask him if he tried on a few flipping hats too?

All this in a flat that wasn't for rent and without bumping into the takeaway staff who were constantly up and down the steps to get supplies. He also managed to ghost through the locked door to the bedsit.

In a brilliant piece of work, our CCTV man Graham worked out the exact moment, from a fleeting piece of white material in the dark on a time lapse camera, when the dumped property had landed with the latex gloves and keys.

From this it was relatively simple to identify the only car passing a nearby traffic camera and get the number. It was a Volkswagen Passat. We tracked it to Luton, via Toddington Services and Naveed admitted he had gone there but denied knowing anything about any property being thrown out.

Also, he said he had sold the car on 8th January when he got back from Luton and didn't remember the name of the buyer. The police national computer was showing it as not registered to anyone.

What we *did* have was a shot of the car going to a Sainsbury's petrol station just after the property was dumped and then pictures of the penniless Naveed, clear as day, going inside and spending about £60 on petrol, cigarettes and snacks. Crucially too, it looked for all the world like there were three people in the car. Then we got the next forensic hit and it was a new name.

A man called Sarwar Gader was the source of a DNA profile from a piece of latex glove found in the street where the keys were dumped. Yes, it was miles from the scene but amazingly a forensic scientist was prepared to say that the piece of glove was a perfect physical fit and material match to the trapped piece of latex glove found in Dogan's leg bindings. The one with Wali Khan's DNA on it.

It was all coming together but now we couldn't find Gader, an Iraqi illegal overstayer. We had a police photo of the bearded Gader and a photo taken from CCTV of another man putting a few pounds worth of fuel in the Passat a few hours before the murder. We had no idea who this was but we did have the name of someone who was listed as a former associate of Gader's on our intelligence system.

I thought he might (a) know where Gader was and (b) be able to identify the other man, a possible fourth person in the gang. I decided to get out and do something useful, with my DS, Tim. I did get restless being in the office and let's face it, you never saw Regan and Carter in a forensic review meeting.

We found this character, still in bed at his house in South Leicester and asked him about Gader. He said he didn't see anything of him anymore but he knew where he lived. I said great, you can tell us but first look at this photo for us and see if you know this other guy. I showed him the CCTV shot.

He looked at photo and then looked at me. Then he looked at Tim. It was as though we were asking him a trick question.

Then he said, '*Well that's Gader isn't it. You know that*'

I looked at the photo and said '*It's not is it? We have a photo of Gader with a beard and I know he could have shaved but it's a different bloke.*'

I had the police photo in my pocket, so I showed it to him. He just laughed.

He said '*They are both Gader. He's lost loads of weight and shaved the beard off and slicked his hair back but that is him*'

Then he tried to tell us where Gader lived but he didn't really know the name of the street so we persuaded him to come for a drive. By the time were in the right area, on the other side of Leicester from where he lived, he had put it all together and realised we were investigating a murder by a group of men and he wanted out. He told us we were on the right street and we needed to work it out from there. I told him it didn't quite work like that.

I said, '*Look you need to point the house out otherwise we'll all get out and start knocking on doors until we find him.*'

Two minutes later we had the house pinpointed and we took him home with our sincere thanks. He just laughed when we dropped him off.

Two days later, while Tom was on his way back from China I think, we nicked Gader at his home and got the most bizarre story from him too. He claimed he *had* gone to a flat above a takeaway shop with Khan and Naveed on the day in question but he only went to the toilet just inside the entrance because he had a bowel problem. He went no further into the building.

He said he could hear some crashing about as he sat there straining and then as he was coming out, they were running towards him down the hall telling him to run, so he ran. He then claimed that in the car one of them passed him a carrier bag full of something and told him to lob it out of the window, so he did.

They were all charged with robbery and murder and the long hard slog to tie up all of the evidence began properly.

We did find the car too. Every couple of days, the OIC for the job, Steve from my team, checked the registration number on the Police National Computer on the off chance that the new owner had now registered it. One day, someone had.

It was over three weeks since the purchase but the buyers were a couple of students in Northants. Steve and I had the same thought at the same time. We had dealt with plenty of students over the years. They didn't clean up much.

We got in touch and they confirmed they had not dusted, vacuumed or washed the car since they had got it. They were happy to assist and let us have the car. On the floor under the back of a driver's seat was a credit card receipt from the takeaway in Lutterworth for £12.40 on 7th January, the evening before the murder.

Jason, of golf trip fame, had been seconded to me as a financial investigator. I asked him to check who the holder of the credit card was. Someone listening asked if I thought the offenders had gone to Lutterworth for some reason, maybe planning the job.

'No', I said. It was better than that. I had had time to think about this and I had worked it out. I told Jason he would find that the owner of the credit card was probably a decent member of the Lutterworth public who wanted a pizza at half six on Saturday evening. He came back to me a bit later and confirmed precisely that.

The receipt was one that Dogan had brought back to Leicester with the Lutterworth takings. This was a golden find. It was evidence that the users of the Passat had been in direct contact with Dogan and/or his bedsit. One of them had inadvertently brought it away from there with him, maybe in the bag of stuff thrown from the car but had not noticed it fall under the front seat of the Passat.

Once the investigation was properly in hand and I had a minute, I organised trip number fifteen. 2012 heralded the return of the Olympic Games to London for the first time in sixty-four years and the return of the Central Area Golf Trip to our favourite location, Bournemouth, after only two.

A couple of major crime boys joined the trip this year for the first time and circumstances dictated that it would be the one and only year for them both. One through a tragic chain of events and the other through, well, embarrassment, I guess.

Spradders was one of the best detectives in the department and my neighbour. He was also one of the most popular and the fittest. He would run miles and cycle even more. He used to curse social cyclists who used namby pamby cycle paths. Real cyclists stayed on the road apparently.

A couple of times I passed him on a fast road between our village and the Leicestershire Police HQ. This road has a perfectly good cycle path and cyclists who don't use it are a menace. I slowed down enough to shout, '*get on the fucking path*!' to him. Naturally, he didn't go anywhere and I got the finger.

He could go on the piss with the best of them and often did but afterwards he would be in the office saying he felt guilty and needed to eat healthily and exercise to make up for the damage.

Sadly, the following year Spradders was taken ill. He was diagnosed with a brain tumour. It was a double whammy for such an active bloke so when he was given the option of a risky operation to sort it out, he went for it with typical courage.

After the op, because I was handily placed for his house, I took him to the Police Rehabilitation Centre in the Home Counties on a couple of occasions, for two week stays designed to help him recover and rebuild. On the way down he talked about not being able to wait to get back on the bike. And when we got there, I had to insist on carrying his bag, over his protests that he could manage now.

After the op he came back to the office and started to do some light duties. Telephone enquiries, that sort of thing. One day, someone asked me if I had noticed anything about him and I had to confess that I had. I thought his speech was getting worse and sometimes it sounded a bit slurred.

Then the news came that tragically and unbelievably he had now got Motor Neurone Disease (MND) too. This is one bastard of an illness which affects the brain and the nerves. There is no cure and about half the people who get it die within three years.

Spradders died in the summer of 2016. He was a hero to us all and one of the bravest men I've ever met. He still retained his sense of humour and his ability to get the right arse with people, until the end.

One day, a few months before we lost him, I was at his house trying to have a conversation with him. He had lost the power of speech by this time and communicated using a keyboard which created a synthesized voice. Like Lost Voice Guy, the comedian. You may have realised if you've seen him on TV, that on these things you can pre-set certain phrases or words in your keyboard if you think you might use them a lot. You know, like *please* and *thank you*.

Anyway, this day I asked him something and as he started to type his answer I stepped to the side of his wheelchair and looked at what he was typing. He snarled at me and hit one of his pre-set buttons. An electronic voice told me to '*FUCK OFF*'. I had done the equivalent of interrupting him as he spoke. His wife Verene just laughed. She had seen it before.

He had plenty of other choice phrases loaded and ready to go. He had also taken to carrying a loaded *Nerf* gun so he could shoot people to attract their attention.

Spradders had previously told me, with a slight smirk, that he blamed me for not getting the brain tumour diagnosis quicker than he did. It was because after the Major Crime Christmas Do that year, he persuaded Verene to pick us both up. We were both arseholed but it is fair to say I was worse than him. Coming out of the pub onto Millstone Lane in Leicester City Centre he said he suddenly felt faint and his legs nearly went from under him for no reason. It scared him but then he looked ahead at me, trying to weave my way towards the car and thought, oh he's doing it as well, it must be the beer.

His funeral was a celebration of a life filled to the brim with action and fun but cut way too short. The Major read his last words which pretty much said *'if you're thinking of doing something please just go and do it while you can'.* Afterwards in the bar at Vipers RFC he found me and said, *'a few pints son then we'll do the boy proud. Top shelf. The Irish and the Scotch.'*

Around 1am the Major had gone and Baras's better half Jean, picked us up and they took me home. I insisted they drop me at the end of a long road about half a mile from my house so I could get some fresh air. I can't remember much more except that I fell in a hedge about halfway home and it took me some time to get out of it.

I have never been near Spradders's league as a runner. All I have done is complete the desk to 5K programme a couple of times to get my arse moving a bit. Once, after his death, I found myself slowing down at the end of a thirty minute jog as I started to go up the hill that leads past his house, around the corner from my own.

I thought about walking but then I could hear him in my head shouting, *'Come on you big jessie. Dig in! Dig in!'*

Legend.

Anyway, back in 2012 he was fit and playing golf off an eighteen handicap.

The other first timer was Jim. He was a detective with similar long service to me in the job. He was an abrasive character who rubbed some people up the wrong way but for whatever reason I always got on with him and he did some excellent work for me. One thing I never had him down for was naivety.

As had happened a couple of times now, on the first night we found ourselves in Spearmint Rhino. I did my usual thing of hanging out with Eddie and the Major and taking advantage of the happy hour beer. Eric was warned to behave or if he couldn't behave, to use cash.

Jim was like a kid in a sweetshop. He had obviously never been anywhere like this before and he did avail himself of a few private dances with a young lady. I don't know how much he spent but at one point he disappeared to an ATM to re stock and despite Spradders telling him to stop, he spent that too.

The next night he was at it again and when we got back to work Spradders took a couple of us to one side and told us Jim had fallen in love with this girl and would not have it that she was only after his cash. He was talking of going back to Bournemouth to meet up with her.

I don't know if he ever did but at some point I think he came to his senses. He did start asking for more overtime later that year and I was only too happy to help out there. He never did ask to come on the trip again though.

One person who had better trips was Mick. I had known him since I got promoted to sergeant in 1996 and he was one of the Whitby originals. He roomed with Thomo and after the first night he looked dreadful. He said Thomo's snoring was so bad that he wouldn't be surprised if you could hear it outside. He tried to wake him up and when that didn't work he went and slept in the bath. Even from there he said it was like a pneumatic drill. He actually thought of going to sleep in Thomo's BMW in the car park at one point.

The walk down to the beach on the first day had not started well for Mick when an idiot cyclist crashed into him in the park we always walked through to get to our favourite bar on the sea front. Mick shouted some very much deserved expletive at the guy who promptly stopped, threw his bike down and started a fight. A few of the lads got in the way before a decent punch was thrown and this character was strongly advised to clear off.

As we stood on the first tee Mick said '*At least I'll be able to get some sleep on the way home tomorrow. He will have to drive.*'

In the event, Thomo's snoring was even worse on the second night. Then, when we all left, Thomo drove for about half an hour before pulling in saying '*You'll have to drive mate. I'm knackered. I've hardly had a wink of sleep.*'

The golf itself was another high scoring event and it sent PD into apoplectic state. Jason got his game together and made a mockery of what was the right call at the time. He had been playing cricket and football but hardly any golf.

He had missed two of the last five trips but in the three he did play, off twenty-one, he got scores in the low twenties. So, I upped him to a twenty-three handicap and he smashed it out of the park with forty points. It was an extremely high scoring event. Alan got thirty-four points but couldn't get into the top five.

Once again though, sunny Bournemouth had been a hit. I went back to concentrate on the Dogan investigation.

Before that, in September I went to London with Katy. With the kids safely looked after we had a two night break to celebrate our twentieth wedding anniversary. As I write we are gaining on thirty years and I am all of a sudden feeling old.

I had met Katy whilst on patrol in uniform in 1989. I was with another mate who is no longer with us, Steve. We stopped her yellow Mark 2 Ford Escort, ostensibly because it had a brake light out (it did) but we had both seen the driver and thought we would like to chat. This sort of thing gets you sacked nowadays.

Four days later I was out on solo patrol when I saw her again, light still defective, '*great I can stop her again*', I thought. I am a smooth bastard it must be said (I'm not) but I got a little bit of encouragement; then she told me she had a boyfriend and had been with him for eight months. Game over.

A few weeks on and I hadn't seen her again but then one morning I was sent to a burglary at a local Peugeot dealership. The salesman who helped me with the crime report was called Dean and once the report was sorted, he made me a brew.

He was nineteen and I was twenty-three and we talked about the things lads of that age talk about. Football, women and where you go out. I told him the story and to my amazement he knew who Katy was and said that they used to be an item.

Not only that he told me that the reason I hadn't seen the yellow Escort was because he had just sold her a blue Renault. He gave me the registration number and wished me luck.

He said, '*I would really love to go out with her again but it's not going to happen and this bloke she is seeing is a total prick. I hope you screw it up for him.*' He also told me where she parked her car when she was at work.

The next time I was with Steve he persuaded me to write a note which he put under her windscreen wipers. We went on our first date about two days later and then she dumped the chump and the rest is history, as someone once said.

Back at work the Dogan Dogan trial went ahead and we found ourselves with a superb barrister. Generally speaking, you get allocated Queen's Counsel for a murder trial but we got a very experienced barrister called Gordon who was not one.

He should have been outgunned by the three QCs representing the defendants but he was not. He played them like a violin. He made them look second rate for most of the trial. Admittedly it is easier when you have evidence of the quality we had provided.

He took each defendant out during detailed forensic cross examinations and his closing speech was masterful. All three defendants turned on each other and all were convicted and handed the same sentence. Life imprisonment with a minimum term to serve of twenty-eight years before an application for parole could be made.

Tom was absent from the six week trial for all but three or four days due to the pressures of the Du investigation. Du was now supposedly in Africa and Tom was flying halfway round the world including to China on multiple occasions, trying to catch the bastard. He did eventually too. It was great work.

A number of us were commended by the High Court Judge presiding and we deserved it but Gordon, in my view, was the man of the match. In the pub I asked him why he wasn't a QC. He was a senior barrister and I knew he must have been recommended for silk.

He said '*Simon, I'm happy doing what I'm doing. And you can't get happier than happy.*'

We drank to that.

Worcester 2013

WE DECIDED it was time to enjoy the races again so I booked us in to a hotel with its own golf course in Worcester. The races were on for our first night.

Alan had a murder trial running at Leicester Crown Court so he told me he would meet us there. That was a job with a difference. A guy had tricked his ex-wife into getting into his car and then driven her to a leafy lane near to Gartree, just outside Leicester.

He had disconnected the passenger airbag and at the last minute he undid her seatbelt and drove into a tree, making sure the main point of impact was the near side. She was killed instantly.

Thanks to some outstanding work from Alan and his team and from medical professionals, who sussed that the driver was faking unconsciousness and injuries at the scene, he was convicted.

That conviction was all in the future for him as the golf trip came around. It was mid-trial and we would get an update when he arrived later in the day.

Once checked in I headed for the hotel bar where quite a few of the boys were assembling. We sat on the balcony and had a few beers. A bit later in he walked, still in his suit. He came over to me and the Major and said, '*I need a word*' and motioned us over to one side.

He said, '*You'll be getting calls so I might as well get this over with and let you get started.*'

I wondered what the hell he had done now. I needn't have worried.

He just looked down and pointed at his shoes. The clown had got dressed and gone to Crown Court as the SIO in charge of a murder trial, in odd shoes. They weren't just a little bit different. The only similarity was that they were more or less the same colour. It still gets mentioned now and again. Plus, I have a photo.

At the races I sought out my next door neighbour Michael the bookie, having established in advance this time that he would be there. Then I called Katy and asked her to pick a horse from the list in the paper at home. She did this and I made a note of the name.

I went off to put a fiver on it and three or four of the boys were immediately suspicious. They thought I'd had a tip from Michael. When I backed it, it was about twelve to one but the bleeder started to go out as soon as I had paid.

The Major waited until two minutes before they came under starters orders and then got a tenner on it at sixteens. It romped home. A few more of the boys had money on it as well. Most of them made more than me.

Lee, presumably a celeb spotter now after his encounter with Chubby Brown, spotted AP McCoy in the VIP enclosure so he and another member of the group blagged their way in and got themselves a photo.

The next day the golf was not particularly memorable. The big surprise was me winning the longest drive contest. As I have said before, I don't hit the ball a long way. Using my three wood, I watched as my ball ran to little more than 200 yards. Crucially though it stayed on the fairway and only two others, both fellow short hitters, did the same. In the land of the blind, the one eyed man is king!

The main event was won by Bingo, who was now on his fourth trip and was playing a lot of golf. He got thirty-five points edging out Lee so nobody could really complain about his handicap. At least not this time.

2013 saw the start of another big job for me. I was at home on my wedding anniversary, 12th September, when I got a text from Steve who was on a late shift. The message told me there was a job in. A stabbing of a male in Leicester with two suspects on the run.

Katy and I were due to celebrate our twenty first wedding anniversary with a meal at a local Marriott Hotel restaurant the next evening. As I left for work in the morning, I told her it was not my team's turn to take the next job so whilst I'd be involved, I'd get away in time to go out.

I walked into the office and saw Steve with our newest recruit, Dave. Or *Slippers* as Steve calls him for reasons I'll explain later. I was aware that there was a heck of a lot of people about, including staff from the other EMSOU forces, Notts, Derby, Lincolnshire and Northants.

'*Can one of you tell me about the job before the briefing*?' I asked.

'*Which one?*' said Steve. '*There are two in now. Five dead including a family of four. The world is coming here.*'

I called Katy and told her I wouldn't be home for the meal that night. Or breakfast.

The stabbing of a man called Antoin Akpom on Kent Street in Leicester around 5pm on Thursday came out of a fracas between him and two other men. Alan had moved on and the DCI who had replaced him, another Simon and a veteran of Major Crime, was called out to deal with it. Antoin died in hospital a short time later. He was a football coach in the local area; well-known and popular.

Simon got a lead on the identity of one of the suspects and all indications suggested that he was on his way to London. Simon took up residence in what is called a 'Silver Control' in a room at Force HQ in Enderby.

This is used when a live operation is running and all efforts are being directed towards dealing with it efficiently. It is a kind of command and intelligence centre that directs the activity required to deal with the situation. Simon was there as the senior detective officer. I had been in the same room, in the same capacity as Simon in 2011, during the hunt for Lawrence, after his first escape.

The team had solid intelligence that this character was now almost in London but later they were given an address for him in Leicester. It was his mother's house but he apparently lived there.

It was now after 1am on the Friday morning and Simon was deciding how to approach the Leicester address and what he would need to do it. Then Ivan, the Force Operations Room Inspector, came into the room and told him he would have to clear out.

There was a house fire, Ivan said, with at least four people trapped. It wasn't looking good.

'*Where's that?*', said Simon, packing his stuff away.

'*Wood Hill*', said Ivan.

'*What number*?' said Simon, now interested, '*One of my suspects lives there.*'

'*Fifty-six*'

'*Oh, OK it's fifty-two where my guy lives.*'

They looked at each other.

Then Simon said, '*Oh shit.*'

Four members of the Taufiq family died that night in the most horrific fashion. Mrs Shehnila Taufiq, her eighteen year old daughter Zainab and her sons Bilal, who was seventeen and Jamal, fifteen.

Simon immediately suspected a link between the two jobs. It was experience and instinct, and he was right.

This was as big as it gets and the head of the whole regional homicide response, a Superintendent called Kate, was put in charge of both jobs. The immediate working theory was that they *could* be linked but they would be investigated separately.

Kate had overall control but she put Matt in charge of the fire and Simon kept the murder of Antoin. I was Matt's deputy. My old DS Tim, who had done the Regan and Carter routine with me on Sarwar Gader's friend, was now an acting DI and he became Simon's deputy.

Staff began to arrive in their droves, some from the other forces, some from Leicester CID departments. Like anywhere, some staff are better than others. Our unit was based on the first floor of the building and my office was closer to the stairs. I realised that everyone was being told just to come to Beaumont Leys, not which job they were going to work on. I made sure everyone who came up the stairs reported to my office first so I had my pick. Simon laughs about it now but he wasn't laughing at the time and he soon put a stop to it, with a few choice words for me personally.

The jobs both progressed quickly at first. Simon got the runner in London swiftly, thanks to an eagle eyed British Transport Police

Community Support Officer, while we got a break in another way. A Tactical Support Group search officer called Jim, someone I knew very well, was tasked to search the front curtilage of the destroyed Taufiq home.

Jim started to sift a pile of rubble that had been swept up underneath the front window of the house. A fire officer saw him and told him he didn't need to do that because it had been checked by them. Like most police officers Jim admired Trumpton for being brave, putting out fires and saving lives. He had no idea how good they were at looking for things. He carried on sifting the rubble, because that's what he had been told to do and thank God he did.

Almost immediately he found a red plastic cigarette lighter and carefully, forensically recovered it. A fire service dog handler called Dave who we knew well and really liked was watching.

Dave was the handler of a brilliant forensic search dog and they were to play a hugely important part in the investigation. Dave was also a trained fire investigation officer. He immediately told Jim that this was a significant find. He said the lighter must have been right there in front of the house the whole time. If it had belonged to the house and had been swept outside with other rubble, it would not be in the good condition it was in.

The lighter was removed and immediately taken for a fast track forensic submission. At the same time two DCs were responding to a call to the incident room from a young man called Porter.

Porter initially gave a false name but then came clean to the operator. He reported that he thought he may have witnessed the arsonists heading towards the scene. He said he had been walking down Wood Hill about 12.30am when he saw three men coming up towards him. He didn't like the look of them, especially when they shouted to him. He thought he was going to be robbed.

He was then quite relieved when one of them just asked for a light. He said he used a disposable lighter and told the guy to keep it. He then walked down the rest of the steep hill and turned left at the bottom where a mate was waiting to give him a lift.

The following day I was walking down the corridor at Beaumont when Matt appeared out of his office and said, '*Come in here.*'

I followed him and Kate was there.

Matt said, '*Guess whose DNA is on the lighter.*'

'*Not Porter?*' I said. It was.

Porter was immediately arrested and when he came in, he gave more or less the same bullshit story. All of his supposed movements before and after his alleged walk down Wood Hill at 12.30 were disproved by CCTV cameras that showed no such thing.

More importantly, a CCTV camera in a school at the foot of Wood Hill showed something else. It was grainy but we had footage of two cars coming down Wood Hill, lights off, stopping briefly alongside each other before four people left the first car and ran up the Hill. The second car backed into a space nearby. There was not a view of whether or not anyone got out of *that* car but we realised later that four more had done so. They too went up Wood Hill.

Less than a minute later a massive explosion could be seen on the screen and three people ran down to where the first car had parked and the car left. Footage from another camera showed four men, at exactly the same time, running like the clappers along an adjoining road and off into a maze of streets beyond.

It looked like eight people had done this. Presumably, Porter and seven others. It did seem though, that only seven had come back down the hill. Where was number eight?

Some brilliant detective work, including some outstanding CCTV analysis, led to the identification of six of the others involved. We had also established that the two cars were a green Toyota Yaris and a blue VW Golf. We knew that the two drivers were called Carter and Mullings.

We arrested all six and got a mixed bag of responses. Four of them answered 'no comment' to all questions but Mullings went on a long winded story that landed him right in the sticky stuff. He initially told us that he had been nowhere near the scene on the night but then changed that to say that his auntie had been driving him around to buy some weed.

Then he changed again and said he was driving, with mates he didn't want to name, but this was much earlier than the fire and they had done nothing wrong.

Then he said '*If you don't believe me get my auntie to check. She has one of those insurance trackers in the car to check on where I go and how fast I'm driving*.'

The interviewing officer said, '*Just say that again please.*'

His solicitor closed his eyes.

We had only just recovered the cars. They had been parked up near an industrial estate in a totally different part of the city. I made a quick enquiry and ended up speaking directly to an investigator at the insurance company, drivelikeagirl.com – yes really.

He and I sat 200 miles apart and simultaneously looked at Google Maps. Other mapping applications are available. He pointed me to a spot at the foot of Wood Hill and confirmed that the Golf had been parked there from just before the fire until about an hour and a half later.

The four running men who had disappeared into the local streets had for some reason run straight past their car and opted to escape on foot. Another CCTV camera showed the Golf being quietly removed some ninety minutes later. It had been parked about fifty yards outside the police cordon.

We had an idea of which of the suspects we thought was in each car at the time of the murders. The Yaris was the first car down Wood Hill, headlights off. We knew the driver was Carter and believed that Porter and a lad called Webb were two of the other three. Carter and Webb were both sticking to their '*no comment*' tactics.

In the other car we had the driver, Mullings, a sixteen year old youth called Parker who actually lived on Wood Hill, plus an ex-Para called Powell and a Leeds Metropolitan University student called Jeffers. Powell was the only other one who was talking.

In fact, throughout the whole process Powell was the only one who ever showed any remorse. He still came up with a bullshit story, saying he had been on Wood Hill with the others to go and smoke weed. He named six of them, including the already charged Porter but he would not name the eighth man, who he said was bad news and scared him.

He said the group of eight were all sauntering up the left hand side of Wood Hill when Porter and the eighth man went across the road and up to the front of the house. Suddenly there was an explosion and everyone ran off, so he ran too, initially back to the Golf but then when Mullings ran past it, they all followed.

He said they made their way across the city and then went their separate ways but Mullings was told he had to go back and get the car. Powell cried like a baby when we discussed the family that had died. He knew that he was going to get charged and when the recording system in the interview room was switched off, he told the interviewers that the eighth man was a guy called Richards.

Powell confirmed that Richards had been in the Yaris with Porter, Carter and Webb but that when their group later saw Carter, he told them that Richards did not escape from the fire with them. He had apparently run *up* the hill. We later learned that this Richards character habitually spent most of his time at his girlfriend's house on a street at the top of Wood Hill. It was a two minute walk from the scene.

In the Yaris, Carter and Porter dropped Webb off at his home. The Yaris turning into and emerging from Webb's street was captured on CCTV. Then the two of them went to a takeaway on Narborough Road, where Carter calmly bought chicken whilst the bodies of an innocent woman and her children still smouldered in their home.

Richards was the only proper criminal in the group. He was best known for being a drug dealer. None of the others had rated much of a mention on police systems and certainly not in the courts. Porter had been cautioned for possession of an offensive weapon, a pen knife. That's why his DNA was on the national database, resulting in the forensic hit on the lighter.

The rest were, at least before 13th September, decent lads with a future. Porter was an outstanding footballer. I hope they sent him to that prison where Vinny Jones runs the football team.

We now had seven people each charged with four murders. We had little evidence on Richards. We arrested him and prepared for the fact that he would go '*no comment*'. We had to decide what we would do to progress the investigation when we failed to get enough to charge him.

In the event though, we couldn't shut him up. The interviewers were Andy and Nick, highly experienced major crime detectives.

Nick was an old friend who had been Grover's partner when they interviewed Russell back in 2003. They did a fantastic job with Richards. These are the highlights:

Immediately after the fire Richards had called or texted six of the other seven suspects. He denied this even when we showed him his own call records.

We also showed him, in a key witness statement supported by call records, that a friend of Porter's had called Porter on Richards's phone two hours before the fire. He refuted this saying he didn't even know Porter and that would be his younger brother borrowing his phone. We proved that his younger brother was in Liverpool at the time.

Richards said he had not left his girlfriend's house between 8pm on the night of the fire and 10am the morning after. We could prove that his phone *had left* and he said it was with him the whole time, conveniently forgetting his earlier lie about his brother.

Throughout the day, as Richards told more and more provable lies, I was phoning our brilliant CPS lawyer, Sam. I kept asking her if we had enough to charge. She kept saying no.

Finally, I tipped her over the edge and she said *'OK Shutts it looks good, charge him. And now please, please just fuck off and let me write it all up, you pain in the arse.'*

As it happens Katy and I had tickets to see Alison Moyet at Warwick Arts Centre that night and I had thought I wouldn't make it. I had told her to start ringing some mates to see if she could find one who wanted to go with her.

When Sam told me to fuck off, I grabbed my stuff, shouted to my DS and two DCs Liz and Julie who had been leant to us by Leicestershire CID *'Charge him and do the file! I'm off to see Alison Moyet! And thanks!'* I ran down the stairs and we made it. Alison was fantastic and we have seen her again since then. Highly recommended.

I have mentioned before that in these cases, an officer in the case or OIC gets appointed from the Major Crime Department. Our newest recruit Dave had been with us for over a year now and was ready for a big job like this.

Ordinarily Dave should have been preparing the charges and doing the file. He had done so for the first seven we charged. This time though he was in Portugal on a stag do, losing his phone, his wallet and his dignity. And it wasn't even *his* stag do. He is a good friend of mine and a DI himself now. The job was to have another turn and a first for the two of us as the investigation progressed.

Dave, a former public schoolboy who knows everything about cricket and nothing about football, had impressed me on his first job as OIC when, with Matt in charge, we locked up the murderer of the boxer Shaun Cummins. When he first joined the team, I gave him to Steve, my oldest DC, to mentor. Steve has many skills including being someone who knows more ridiculous words in online *Scrabble* than any other living person. Discretion though, is not a natural quality he is blessed with.

Steve, now retired, was *old school* and he remembered when things were done in a certain way. As we know, many such things have changed for the better now but some standards have slipped. One day the two of them had been out on an enquiry somewhere in torrential rain. They came in utterly drenched and Steve immediately took his shoes and socks off and put the socks on a radiator. He then walked round barefoot, trying to persuade someone else to make the tea, as was his habit.

My own office was a small space off the main team office and I came out of it at Steve's request. He invited me to look down. It is important at this juncture to point out that Dave is a self-confessed clothes horse. His theme tune, if he had one, would be *Dedicated Follower of Fashion* by *The Kinks*. He owned seven suits at the time and any one of them was worth more than all four of Steve's put together.

I looked down and he was wearing a trendy little pair of *Saville Row* moccasin slippers. Steve was just standing there with his arms folded, shaking his head, like one of those Les Dawson washer women gossips at the garden fence.

I said, '*David, I'm going to the toilet. When I come back, they will not be on your feet. You are a detective now. Not a prefect at Rugby School.*' Standards.

As far as I know the offending footwear spent the rest of its natural life in a drawer underneath Dave's desk, although I do have a faint memory of seeing one of them on the sloping roof beneath the office window. If ever Steve mentions Dave in a text to me these days, he just refers to him as '*Slippers*'.

Anyway, sorry I did a Ronnie Corbett again there, but back to the investigation. We were amassing a wealth of circumstantial evidence which we felt was quite damning for the defendants. We had the CCTV of Carter and Porter in the takeaway fifteen minutes after the fire but two of the four in the Golf, Jeffers and Parker, never spoke to us in interview. We would have to prove to a jury that they were there at all.

The word of a co-accused like Powell is worth little. The footage of the four running away was not bad but a positive ID from it would be tricky.

Then our CCTV man, Graham made another of his great discoveries. This was the same person who had done the amazing piece of work with the items being thrown from the car in the Dogan Dogan murder.

Graham had a good knowledge of camera locations in Leicester. We knew that only one of the four had come back to the VW and that was an hour and a half later so it was likely that

they could all have a got a long way away. It looked like there had been some discussion with the other group so maybe they went right through the city, from the east to the west of Leicester.

New Walk is a wide footpath, a little over a mile in length, running right into the city centre. It dates back to 1785 when it was originally called Queens Walk after Queen Charlotte, consort of King George III. A number of high end residences were built on it through the Georgian and Victorian eras. Many of these are businesses now. It retains its *no pedal cycles* status and in parts is still very picturesque with some bars and cafés, as well as Leicester Museum situated on it. *That said*, the green next to the museum is usually populated by people wearing tracksuit bottoms with slip on shoes and drinking cider at ten in the morning.

It would have taken the four runners, assuming they slowed down and walked, about twenty-five minutes to get to New Walk but once there this was the gateway to the west side of the city. Graham took a punt, went to the control centre which covered the New Walk CCTV and recovered the footage from the relevant time. He got back to the yard at Beaumont at 9pm one night, just as Matt and I were leaving.

He told us we needed to see this. It was a nine. A nine was perfect. Graham didn't do tens.

We watched in amazement as, less than an hour after the fire, the VW Golf Crew walked down New Walk. All immediately identifiable in full colour. *Jeffers, Parker, Mullings and Powell.* Laughing, chatting and joking. At one point Mullings, wearing a two-tone tracksuit top and shorts, can be seen to sniff his hands. It became known in the office as the *Reservoir Dogs* clip.

The pictures of Mullings's distinctive top became even more significant later when a witness from a street called Gamekeepers Court, called in to say that he had a CCTV camera outside his house to record local yobs who cause damage and smoke drugs. His routine would be to call the local beat officer if he had anything to complain about.

On this occasion he had footage of a blue VW Golf stopping in the cul-de-sac outside his house a couple of hours after the Reservoir Dogs clip. We recovered it and had a look. The driver, clearly Mullings, could be seen to get out, go to the boot and remove something. He then took whatever the item was into some bushes and emerged empty handed. Someone else was clearly visible in the front passenger seat. The CCTV was from about two hours after the fire.

Before calling the police, the witness had bravely sent his wife into the bushes to see what was there. It was a brand new, bright green plastic petrol can, almost full of petrol.

Of course, we now had a full record of the movements of the Golf, with the tracker recording a hit every time it stopped or started and, in any case, every thirty minutes. We didn't always find out why the car had been to certain places but this was one explained.

As we now had full colour footage of six of the group and had recovered *all* their clothing when searching their houses, we now had things to look for. We found very little and this was later put to the jury as suspicious. Porter's Miami T-shirt, Parker's Nike Air T-shirt, Mullings's two tone tracksuit top and Jeffers's jacket with the white logo on the back were nowhere to be found. They had all been disposed of.

Carter never got the memo though. He apparently loved his Champion sweatshirt too much. He lived in a multi-room hostel and obviously thought we would only search his room. He was wrong. In the loft, in a dark little cupboard blocked in by some furniture was the sweatshirt, freshly laundered, in a carrier bag.

Actually, the evidential value of it was limited but for the fact that he had hidden it. All of the disposed kit was much better.

Similarly, they all had issues with the phones they had used on the night. They had remembered to switch them off as they left their gathering point in the west of the city, before their two-car convoy over to Wood Hill. Later though we had a right collection of nonsense from them. All of them had done one or more of the following: Deleted data, deleted the device phone book, changed the number, made suspicious dictionary entries searching for information about the crime, or in the case of four of them, lost the phone completely.

One who had not lost his phone was Aaron Webb. We were satisfied that we had got the phone he had used on the night but we couldn't get into it. It seems silly now, it was an iPhone 4S and nobody we tried could crack it. All police forces have the kit to get into any phone these days but back then it was different. Webb had refused point blank to give us the pin code.

I went to the national Senior Investigating Officers Conference in November, in search of the answer. These events have three days of guest speakers plus evening soirees which at your first conference are funny and entertaining but after three or four have lost their gloss. I did five.

One other thing the conferences have is sponsorship. This means there are always exhibition halls full of service providers selling all kinds of things, often of a hi-tec nature like mini DNA labs and new intelligence collection systems. And to tempt people in they have bags, benches and boxes full of free stuff to give away.

The delegates, largely DIs and DCIs with no authority or budget to buy any of this kit, wander round pretending they *do* have such authority whilst really just trying to blag free stuff and entering every competition going, of which there are several.

In fact, one of our Derbyshire EMSOU brethren won a new iPad one year but was still too shitfaced on the final morning to walk up and collect it from the front. Did I mention there was a bar?

I have had pens, USBs, mugs, sweets, corkscrews and cool bags to name just a few things. Three of our big thermos coffee mugs, still in use at home, have *Slater and Gordon Solicitors* on the side. So does one of our shopping bags.

Getting back to the point, when I attended the conference in November 2013, I trawled the stands of all the communications companies. All of them told me there was not a firm in the UK that could get into a password protected iPhone 4S.

Early in 2014, I tried another approach. I could not believe that this could not be done. There was a government communications team in London who were part of the national security network. I gave them a call and spoke to a bloke who gave me the same old story.

I was fairly sure that if Webb had blown up a double decker bus, they'd have got into his phone but I didn't say that. Instead, I said I would phone the Americans and see what they could do. The phone was made in California after all. The Yanks were bound to have experienced the same issues.

To my surprise this guy got quite grumpy and told me that his department were the national liaison people for the USA and any contact would have to come through them. Not plebs like a lowly DI on a homicide team. He didn't use those words but that's how I took it.

I finished the call, gave it ten minutes, then called the San Francisco Homicide Detail. San Jose is actually closer to Apple in Cupertino but I had been to San Francisco on holiday and thought San Jose would be a backwater by comparison. Actually, it is bigger. Anyway, I called the SFPD, home of Inspector Dirty Harry Callaghan.

Within five minutes of talking to a Detective Sergeant in Homicide I knew that you could get a federal warrant and ask Apple to break into any phone. They apparently made you jump through several hoops but would then do it all for free. In the UK, this kind of service when they *can* do it, is expensive. All it needed was for someone to take the phone to Apple in Cupertino, CA. Hmmm.

I put this thought to Sam from CPS who had stopped swearing at me by now. In fact we got on really well. She has a fantastic sense of humour and no time for '*knob heads*', as she put it. She told me, modest as she is, to write in this book that she was the best CPS lawyer I ever worked with. It is an easy one to agree to because she was. It wasn't even close and I know that is a view shared by many others, including Kate.

In my experience, some CPS lawyers grow a kind of risk aversion cell in their bodies and will not authorise charges if they think there is a chance they might lose. Sam was no pushover, as can be seen by the seven calls I had to make to her, trying to get Richards charged. The difference between Sam and many of her peers though was that she would take a measured risk and she could always see the big picture and what was best for the investigation. Plus, she wanted all the *knob heads* locked up.

I worked with other good CPS solicitors for sure. Alison, who was our lawyer on the Dogan Dogan case was one of these. Positive and a lovely person. And Cath who was our lawyer way back on the Russell job was the same. Some others, only a few, I had issues with. As an area DI working in Loughborough, I gained a reputation as someone that officers would come to if the duty CPS lawyer had refused to charge the person they had arrested. In one case a group of lads had been playing a semi-organised football match on a local pitch when it was invaded by some local morons, intent on a fight. They were older and bigger than the footballers and four of them ended up getting arrested for assault.

The worst of these was a man who had broken the cheekbone of one of the young boys by kicking him in the face. The lad himself identified the offender by picking him out of an identity parade so that was a good start. The Loughborough uniformed cops dealing with it did a great job and took some detailed statements. One of these statements, the duty lawyer said, was so contradictory she was not going to authorise a charge. She said that the best witness, an adult walking his dog past the pitch, had described the man who kicked the boy in the face as wearing a Red Madrid football shirt but the suspect, who was arrested ten minutes later, was actually wearing a white shirt.

The officers came to see me and I looked at the statement. Straight away I could see that she had cocked it up. Maybe it was because me and the dog walker were football fans or maybe I was just better at reading the handwriting of police officers, I don't know.

I went up to her room and said '*Sorry, I think you've made a mistake. This witness does not say 'red Madrid football shirt', he says 'Real Madrid football shirt'. Real Madrid play in white. That gives you the victim and a brilliant independent witness. Plus, the guy was arrested nearby ten minutes later in a Real Madrid shirt. The job's a good 'un. Can you authorise it now please?*'

To my astonishment she refused. She said she had made her decision and could not change it. I was bloody furious. The poor boy had got a smashed in face and the rest of his childhood would probably be affected, let alone how much pain he would be in and how much more he would have to go through. This woman did not give a flying fuck about that and she was refusing to charge the other three yobs for various other poor reasons too.

I appealed it to three more lawyers at Leicester CPS. The first two were not willing to go against their colleague but the third, Godfrey, called me. He was technically their boss. He asked me how many times I was going to appeal this case. I told him I'd keep going until one of them charged the idiot. Godfrey told me he envied me because I was a DI and if I told a sergeant or a constable what to do, they did it. He said that he might be the head of his CPS unit but if he told another senior lawyer that he or she had got a decision wrong they just told him to fuck off.

In this case he took the matter on himself rather than try to tell the woman she had made a mistake and get the usual mouthful. He said he would charge all four suspects and he bet me fifty pence per defendant that they would all be found not guilty. At their first magistrates court appearance, before any trial, three of them made early guilty pleas. A week later the fourth one joined in and they were all sentenced in the crown court. A week later, a CPS courier came to my office and handed me three pound coins with a note from Godfrey. He had upped the winnings to an amount I could buy a pint with!

I had numerous run-ins with the CPS after that and I didn't always persuade them to change their minds but many of them were good people and not as obtuse as Red Madrid woman and they were willing to listen to a reasoned argument. Clearly, many of the cases that officers brought to me were ones in which I had to explain that I agreed with the CPS decision but 100% of the cases I persuaded them to change their decision and charge on, led to convictions. Some were for minor matters compared to murder but it still represents some of the work I'm most proud of. Victims should come first, not second, to the reputation of the CPS or the police.

Anyway, sorry about that rant. Back on the Wood Hill fire case in 2014, Sam's view was that if Richard, our QC, said the USA trip was necessary, she would write the International Letter of Request (ILOR). This is a complicated and very formal document under the Mutual Legal Assistance Treaty, asking the Americans for permission for me to go over and do investigative stuff.

We had been lucky to get Richard. He was without exaggeration one of the top ten criminal barristers in the country. And he was an absolute gent. He once ripped me to shreds in the witness box when he was on the other side in a murder trial but he did it ever so politely.

He came with his trusty sidekick James, a very experienced barrister in his own right and now a top QC himself. I am pleased to count James as a friend these days and like Richard he is so courteous. Dave and I managed to get out for a beer and a curry with James ten days before Boris first appeared on TV to tell us all to Stay Home, Stay Safe and Protect the NHS. My last such beer for a few months.

Back in 2014 Richard thought the visit to Apple absolutely had to be done. So, at the beginning of March Dave and I, armed with all the requisite paperwork, diplomatic visas and Webb's phone, boarded a jet to San Francisco. We were set to meet a DS from Homicide, Gary, who would take us to our hotel.

The appointment with Apple was two days hence and Gary had told us not to book flights home for two days after that because Apple had a habit of postponing and telling you to come back the next day.

As we came in for landing, Dave said '*I think I'll hit the gym, have something to eat and get my head down.*'

'*Dave*', I said. '*We're going to the pub.*'

The captain told us on approach that the co-pilot would be taking us in to land. We hit the ground with a massive bump and flew back up in the air before he got control of it and despite a slightly swervy second attempt, got us there safely. Dave fancied a drink too after that. It was his first long haul trip and I told him, no, that landing wasn't normal.

Gary picked us up and looked after us for the entire trip including taking us to Apple. I had to respond to an e-mail from them on arrival in the US which if left unanswered meant they would cancel. We also had to arrive bang on time. If you are more than five minutes late, they cancel.

On our first night though, after a few beers, Gary took us to an Italian restaurant called Pinocchio and left us, as he had another commitment. He knew the head waiter and as a result we were treated like royalty. The owner was called Giovanni. We ended up sitting at the bar talking to him and the barman, whilst eating homemade gnocchi, the like of which I have never tasted since.

Giovanni by the way, is in that select group of people who have completed the swim from the infamous Alcatraz prison to the shore. Not while it was open, I should add. It was part of a swimming club event, so whilst not quite like Clint Eastwood with a float made from raincoats, it was still a hugely impressive feat.

One thing a CID officer knows about is a leaving do. Detectives have them when somebody moves office. In Pinocchio, the barman we made friends with was on his last ever shift. We were back the following night for his do, another lavish affair with beer, wine and food in great supply.

The Apple trip went without a hitch. We took no chances. Gary drove us there and we were sitting in a diner across the road ninety minutes before our 9am appointment. We met an FBI agent in the

Apple foyer and were escorted to the office of a senior tech person called Dallas. He had a strange office with a desk he stood at and no chair. We gave him the phone and a portable hard drive and he downloaded the entire contents in four minutes. The only other things in the office were a bottle of expensive looking gin and a t-shirt with the many expressions of Darth Vader on it.

Less than an hour later we were at the regional FBI lab where they decrypted the download and we could see texts that showed Webb had left home in distress having heard that Antoin had been murdered. His mum sent him messages begging him not to do anything stupid. He had also deleted the contact details of his co-accused mates before we arrested him. Later at trial, he would be forced to admit that all of this incriminated him.

Before we went to trial, the Antoin Akpom murder trial took place in Stafford. Simon's team had located the second suspect in hiding in Cardiff. His name is Hussein Hussein and he had been relocated to Leicester from London for some gang-related reason. Antoin paid the price for that shit decision.

The crown's case was that whilst Hussein wielded the knife that was used to kill Antoin, Hakim was still culpable by joint enterprise. The jury disagreed and could not reach a verdict on him.

Hussein was convicted and got life with a joke of a tariff. Fifteen years. The crown later appealed and thankfully won. Hussein's tariff was upped to a minimum of twenty-two years to serve.

Our trial went exceptionally well. Richard was in a class of his own. There were eighteen barristers in that room, our two and two for each defendant. James was the second best there by a country mile.

By this time, another person we had got to know well was Dr Taufiq-a-Sattar, husband and father of the victims. He is a devout Muslim and a neurosurgeon who was working in Dublin at the time of the fire. He got wind of it on the night and phoned in. Matt was forced to tell him on the phone that his wife and family were dead. It was truly horrendous. We all grew to believe that *the Doctor*, as we called him, was an exceptional man.

An example of his character was when he overheard somebody ask me if I had heard that Spradders had a brain tumour. This was well before his MND was spotted.

Spradders was not completely happy with his consultant at the time and Dr Taufiq, with everything he had going on, held a consultation with him in my office at Beaumont, looking at his scans on my desktop computer and advising him on the way forward.

In court he insisted on being present for almost everything although our brilliant Family Liaison Officer, a detective on my team called Karen, conveniently managed to need to speak to him outside at a couple of particularly distressing court moments.

In trials like this, for all of the tragedy and heartbreak, you still have the most ridiculous comedy moments. Without them I think we would all go under. One afternoon a youth came into the public seating area, some of which we had commandeered for us and the Doctor, some was taken by the families of the defendants and most of the rest was the press. This lad was a pain in the arse. He moved from one seat to another and sidled up to different people, none of whom were interested.

After five minutes of him making little noises and constantly moving I made eye contact with him and signalled him to go out. Outside the court I gave him a right bollocking and told him to clear off. He was about eighteen and he didn't react well. In fact, he started crying. I watched him walk away, down the stairs and out of the building.

If only I had searched the little bastard, I might have found the mobile phone he had just nicked from the brother of one of the defendants. Not to worry, none of the team mentioned it much after the first three or four years.

It became apparent early on that this would be a cutthroat defence. This is the term used when a defendant pleads not guilty and piles the blame onto another defendant. The throat being cut by many of those on this indictment belonged to Tristan Richards.

Seven of the eight defendants elected to give evidence. The youth Parker did not. Four of them said they had gone there to smash windows in revenge for the attack on Antoin but knew nothing of a plan to start a fire.

Porter was one of these, having ditched the story about lending three random men his lighter. He now claimed his DNA was on the lighter because he lent it to Richards not knowing what he would do with it.

Four of the others also blamed Richards as the ringleader who planned the job and poured the petrol. Some also pointed out that Porter crossed the road with him and went right up to the house while they were just getting ready to throw stones. The lighter was damning for him after that evidence. Well done Jim.

Dave the dog handler and indeed his trusty hound Freckle did a great job. They found evidence of pooling of an accelerant inside the hall. This meant that the person pouring the petrol had tipped it through the letterbox, effectively condemning the Taufiqs' to death.

The jury were invited to consider where they would expect the family to be at one in the morning. The answer was obvious. Upstairs, stranded.

One of the fire officers gave evidence and said it was, "*one of the most ferocious property fires I have attended...... I remember that the heat that was being vented out was amazing.... the worst domestic fire I have attended in fifteen years.*"

Those same members of the Leicestershire Fire & Rescue Service found the bodies. Not all of them got over that experience.

Richards was the one person saying he was nowhere near Wood Hill on the night and that everyone else was lying about that. As defendant number one Porter had been the first to stick it to Richards in his evidence-in-chief.

Porter wanted to be part of the window bricking gang but some of the boys were turning on him as well as Richards. When the first of this group was cross-examined, Porter's barrister tried to have a go at him but all he managed was to cause hysterics in the court. It was another highly inappropriate moment of comedy when there was nothing to laugh at.

He said *'I see you've fingered Richards then'*

Reply '*Er, yes.*'

The tittering started.

'Well, I put it to you that you only fingered Richards because my client fingered him first?'

I think there was an answer but I don't know what it was and given that he had to leave the room, neither does Dave.

Mullings, our confused driver of the VW Golf, decided to throw himself on the mercy of the court. He told the jury he was a liar. He admitted that he had told lies in his police interview.

'I told numerous lies,' he said. *'It was a cowardly and stupid thing to do but I felt in these circumstances I had to lie.'*

Mulllings also admitted he could be seen on CCTV disposing of a petrol can after the fire but said it had nothing to do with the blaze.

'It had been in my boot for several days as a precaution,' he said.

Now though he wanted to tell the truth. He was adamant he knew of no plan to firebomb the house and he truly had not realised his lights were off as he drove down Wood Hill.

Richard our QC had to wait for seven cross-examinations of each defendant before he got a crack at each one.

He looked at Mullings when it was his turn, *'Mr Mullings, you have told the jury that you didn't know your headlights were off as you drove down Wood Hill, correct?'*

'Yes sir.'

'And you didn't know about the plan to firebomb the house?'

'That's right sir.'

'But what are you?'

'Pardon?'

'What are you Mr Mullings?'

'I don't understand sir, I'm sorry.'

'You're a liar! You told us so yourself earlier today, did you not?'

Jeffers, the university student, gave probably the most bizarre account of all. He said he was with the group and they were going to Parker's house. Parker lived at the top of Wood Hill, 200 yards away.

He knew nothing of any plan to exact revenge on Antoin. He knew who Tristan Richards was but he didn't see him on Wood Hill at any point.

Suddenly there was a bang and everyone ran off. He hadn't been able to see whoever caused this bang because he was just walking past a van at that point, on the opposite pavement, and it blocked his view. He was of course aware afterwards that something had happened because there was a house on fire. This wasn't normal.

Cue Richard.

'So, Mr Jeffers you are in fact just a member of the public who was in the wrong place at the wrong time when criminals you can't identify firebombed a house?'

'That's right yes.'

'You saw that the house was on fire but there was nothing you could do by then so you ran because everyone else ran, yes?'

'Yes.'

'So as a member of the public you must surely have done what any other member of the public would have done on seeing a house explode and catch fire. Let's see. Did you call the fire brigade?'

'No'

'The police?'

'No but – '

'Did you shout for help?

'No.'

'Run to the rescue?'

'No.'

'Detain any of the obvious offenders? No. You didn't and maybe you were scared so in that case you would have called the police later. Did you do that?'

'No.'

'No further questions.'

Richard didn't ask him why. There was no point.

Writing this now I can't remember how long the jury were out for. It was a couple of days as I recall.

Then, one afternoon they came back in and told the judge that all twelve of them could not agree on the charge of murder for all eight defendants. Ultimately the judge said he would accept unanimous verdicts on those defendants they *did* have a decision on and majority verdicts on which no fewer than ten were agreed, for the rest.

He reminded them that the alternative charge of manslaughter was available to them as well.

We all filed out but the jury obviously already knew where this left them and only went outside to double check with each other before coming straight back in.

This was Dave's second murder trial as OIC and he was what I had been at the Russell trial - the proverbial shitting dog. I wasn't exactly calmness personified myself but I was in control. I had been here before. Kate, Matt and Karen were all present amongst others. Karen, who did as perfect a job as a Family Liaison Officer as I have ever seen, was sitting right next to the dignified presence of the Doctor.

The jury returned unanimous verdicts of guilty to the charge of murder for Richards and Porter. They found the other six guilty of manslaughter, all by majority verdict, except for some reason Carter, the driver of the Yaris, who got a unanimous vote.

The judge, Mr Justice Griffiths-Williams, made his views quite clear, saying, '*The horror of what [then] happened is all too apparent. The quantity of petrol and the pouring of petrol through the letterbox provide the evidence the plan was that the house was to be consumed by fire, which took hold instantly and spread upstairs.*'

The judge was in no doubt that Richards was the mastermind and the motivation of the crime.

He said '*You, Richards were the ringleader. I have no doubt that yours was the dominant role. You acquired the petrol and you led the other defendants to the house.*'

He sentenced Richards to life imprisonment with a minimum term of thirty-five years. He was twenty-three at the time. He will not get out until he is fifty-eight, if he gets out then.

Porter was given short shrift by the judge too.

He said, '*Although you acted under the influence of Richards you knew full well what the consequences of your action would be. You had opportunities to dissociate yourself from the plan but you did not.*'

Porter was handed life with twenty-five years minimum. He was nineteen. His life is in tatters.

I write that with no joy or satisfaction, except in the fact that we made sure those responsible were brought to justice. Many people had their lives ruined from these events. Dr Taufiq, Antoin's family but also the families of those who committed the crimes. Most of them were decent people.

The others got a mixture of lengths of determinate sentences. The two drivers got fifteen years. Three of the others got twelve years and Parker, by then aged seventeen, got eight years. Personally, I thought that was lenient: He had not given evidence and the jury had heard two of his co-accused tell the court that he, as a Wood Hill resident, had been asked which house it was by Richards and he had pointed it out. Aaron Webb had told the court that this did *not* happen and that Parker had told Richards he did *not* know which house it was but the judge rejected that, calling it '*frankly incredible*'.

As I type, I know that Parker has been out for some time and must assume that Webb, Jeffers and Powell are as well. The drivers will not be far behind and may already be out on tag somewhere or doing easy time in an open prison.

At Nottingham Crown Court on 24th June 2014, the Doctor had the last word and nobody who was there to hear it will ever forget it.

He said, '*I cannot say that I am living. I merely exist. I am like a brutally wounded bird with no wings.*'

Never before, or since, did I work on an investigation where the names of the victims came up in the actual enquiries so infrequently.

The Taufiq family had nothing whatsoever to do with the senseless murder of a popular football coach in Leicester on 12th September 2013.

But they died because of it.

Bournemouth 2014

I DIDN'T know it at the time but we were well into the back nine of the golf trip story.

I travelled down to our number one venue with the Major, Alan and Baras. We arrived around lunchtime and meeting up with some more of the twenty-two strong group we headed for our favourite bar, Hot Rocks, overlooking the beach and the pier.

We had two or three pints and the remainder of the group gradually wandered in. Eddie and Greg were late arriving, which is just as well, or I am sure Eddie would have got involved in what happened next.

The Major announced that he was going for a dip. He had had about four pints and a plate of chips and was hardly in the best condition but we thought he just meant *a dip,* so we let him get on with it.

Then as he made his way over to the foot of the pier, he announced that he was going to swim to the end. Before anyone could stop him he was off, plunging into the surf like Johnny Weissmuller in Tarzan. Except Johnny had the edge as a swimmer and marginally the better physique.

We had a clear view and we watched as he battled the surf. We lost sight of him for two or three seconds a couple of times but he always re-appeared and battled on. The tide was strong though and after what seemed like a long time, he had only struggled out about thirty yards.

Then he disappeared again but this time – nothing. Alan takes the piss now but I saw his reaction and he was properly worried. There was little point any of us going in after him so we sent the only option: Jamie.

Jamie was on every trip from 2006 to the end. He is even older than me (well by fifteen days) but quite a lot fitter. He cycled to several of the trip venues over the years including Bournemouth and Reading, which most of the group thought was bonkers but he doesn't care. It's more fun than driving and it is not as far as biking from John O'Groats to Lands' End, which he has also done.

Jamie set off down the beach in his flip flops and was preparing to jump in when we all saw a fracas at the far end of the pier. The Major was there holding his hands aloft victoriously and waving to us in the bar. We saw him start to walk up the pier towards the entrance, so Alan and I walked over to meet him and Jamie came up from the beach too. As we got there he was just coming out of the gate.

'Did it!' he shouted *'Oh ye of little faith! Bit dodgy towards the end when I scraped the bottom though.'* He indicated towards his leg which was scratched to buggery. His feet too were bleeding profusely.

Oddly two security guards were standing just behind him as he walked towards us. I went over and spoke to them. I asked one of them if he had come up the steps at the end of the pier, not really knowing if there *were* any steps at the end of the pier.

'Did he fuck,' said the guard. *'We saw the silly twat floundering about a quarter of the way out and yelled at him to turn back but he was all in. In the end we went down a hatch and accessed some steps underneath to let him up.'*

'How come we saw him waving from the end then?' I asked.

'Because he asked us to let him. We told him he'd got two minutes and now we've told him to get off the pier and not come back', he said.

'Oh, and he cut his feet on the barnacles on the steps he came up. Not the fucking seabed!'

On the course the next day I cut Bingo to fifteen. I knew he had been playing a lot and there was no way he was having eighteen again. It didn't matter because he played to thirteen and won anyway. It was Alan's best ever chance too; he was second, separated from the limping Major only on countback.

Lee managed to get himself into more trouble on the course than anyone else did off it. Halfway round the Meyrick Park course there is a wall behind which there are some nice houses. Lee can be a bit wayward and he hits the ball a long way. He managed to smash one over the wall and straight through a window in one of the houses.

He found a way into the garden and met the owner, offering to pay for the damage but she didn't want him to. She said it wasn't the first time. Lee was heading for what, for him, was a woeful total of eighteen points. By the eighteenth tee he had had enough and going up the left hand side of the final hole he had another wayward moment. This time he cleared the high boundary and sent his ball sailing over the ineffectual wire mesh and with a hop, skip and a jump, smashing through the back window of an Audi. Time for bed Zebedee.

Being a good lad, Lee went to the Pro Shop and saw one of the assistant professionals. He told him what had happened. This young lad said not to worry, it had happened before, it would probably happen again. He told Lee that it was rare for someone to come in and be honest about it. Usually they had no idea who had done what.

Room wise, I was sharing with the Major. Half an hour after I came off the course I was sitting on my bed, on the phone to Katy when she asked if he was OK. I said I didn't know because he was off somewhere preparing his speech for after the presentations. He hadn't told me who was going to be the subject of one of his Hans Christian Andersen stories. I was just hoping it wouldn't be me this year.

All of sudden, he burst in and threw a pile of wood on the floor, along with a big sheet of polythene and some other junk. God knows where he got it all from. I told Katy what I was looking at and said I had no idea what he was doing.

Next, he arranged the pieces of wood into a cross and wrapped the polythene round them, securing it all with string. And then I knew who the target was. It was Lee.

'He's making a window' I said.

Bournemouth 2015

THE 2015 trip was uneventful and was won again by Bingo. I cut him by a couple more shots but it wasn't enough and he incurred my displeasure later when someone told me he had said, *'I've had Shutts's pants down. I could have won it off ten. I've been playing that well.'* I parked that one for another day.

At lunchtime, I would always try to organise it so that the boys coming off could walk into the clubhouse and get stuck straight into chips and sandwiches. Some of them would only have forty-five minutes before they were out again for another eighteen holes.

I had just filled my plate up when one of the bar staff told me the manager wanted a word. I went through and saw this chap who was not best pleased.

'I've had some complaints that someone has been repeatedly blowing a bugle' he said.

I just looked at him. Poker face time. '*OK. Should this mean something to me*?' I asked.

'*Well, is it one of your group*?' he said.

'*We are playing golf mate. Not always very well. Why would one of us be playing a trumpet*?'

'*It's a bugle*'

'*OK if you say so. None of that lot could play a triangle.*'

'*Oh. All right*' he said. '*Sorry then.*'

As I walked back in hoping there were some chips left, I saw the culprit.

'Eddie!!'

Back in Leicester and I had started 2015 by completing a six-month stint as a temporary DCI, heading up the Leicestershire part of EMSOU Major Crime. In all that time I didn't pick up a single new murder investigation.

As soon as my acting up ended and I was back to being a DI, I started getting jobs. I had graduated now to be the SIO on my jobs rather than the deputy.

But it was another massive investigation in which I would once again be the number two to Kate, which would occupy my time from November 2015. This lasted for seven months to trial and then indirectly would still be providing me with work after my retirement at the end of 2017.

Kate remained the head of EMSOU-Major Crime throughout 2015. She has since gone up through the ranks and is now a chief officer. She was usually a quietly spoken and modest person and she was an outstanding senior detective. Before the Wood Hill fire, as a DCI she led the investigation into the deaths of six young children in a house fire in Derby. It was an horrific job. The main perpetrator although three people were convicted, was the loathsome father of the children, Mick Philpott. Richard the eminent QC, James his brilliant number two and Sam from CPS had all worked with Kate on that job too.

Leicestershire provided about ten long term staff to the Philpott investigation and they were impressed with this Nottinghamshire SIO, leading a Derby job. One thing they did say though was don't upset her and don't let her catch you slacking off. When she exploded you were best off being somewhere else.

One day on the Wood Hill job in 2013 she said she was going to take a joint briefing of our staff on the fire and Simon's staff on the Antoin Akpom investigation. I was standing next to Matt when she came in. Somebody or something had incurred her displeasure and she ripped into the room. Her eyes were blazing. She made it quite clear that if there were people there who were not prepared to put the hard yards in or who were going to cut corners and not do the job properly, then they should leave.

Natural instinct is to worry that it might be you. I was standing next to Matt and he must have seen the look on my face. He smiled. He already knew what it was about.

'*Don't worry son, it's not us*' he whispered. Phew.

It was actually an idiot of a DC on Simon's team who had completely ruined the evidence of an eyewitness to Antoin's stabbing. Simon was even more angry than Kate. The DC was not a Leicestershire officer and he was later sacked from the police for some other misbehaviour, back in the force he had come from.

Back to 2015. I got an early call telling me to get myself in for 7am rather than my habitual 8.30. When I arrived Kate was already there, as was Martin, a Newcastle United supporting, Lincolnshire DCI I always got on really well with. We had a missing teenage girl.

Kayleigh Haywood was fifteen and the day before we got involved, her Mum reported her missing. Early on that Sunday morning a builder was driving along the A447 in the village of Ibstock in Leicestershire. Before it enters the main part of the village, the road reaches a point where it bends and has the huge Sence Valley Forest Park on one side and a small and, at the time, very new housing estate on the other.

Just as he reached that point the builder saw what he thought was a phone in the road. He stopped and picked it up. It was an iPhone with a smashed screen. He couldn't get past the pin code but he did manage to call the last number to have contacted the phone as it was displayed on the screen.

The number belonged to a friend of Kayleigh's. The friend lived right there in Ibstock but Kayleigh lived in the village of Measham, just over five miles away. The friend met the builder and took the phone. She then called Kayleigh's mum.

Kayleigh's mum Stephanie was confused. Kayleigh had asked permission to go and stay the Friday and the Saturday night with the friend who was now calling her to ask where Kayleigh was on Sunday morning. They were both supposed to be at this girl's adult sister's home in Ibstock.

The friend knew nothing about this arrangement and said she had last seen Kayleigh at school on Friday. Stephanie called the police.

The first officers to arrive completed the usual tasks for a missing person investigation to commence and had the presence of mind to ask Stephanie about Kayleigh's social media activity.

Stephanie said Kayleigh was always either texting or on Facebook. She knew the password and logged in. She was not prepared for what she saw. Over the previous two weeks Kayleigh had exchanged a huge quantity of messages with a man called Harlow in Ibstock. Neither Stephanie nor Kayleigh's dad Martin had ever heard of Harlow.

The messages clearly showed that Kayleigh had arranged to go and stay the night with Harlow on Friday 13th November. The story about staying with a friend was a ruse. In fact, Stephanie said that Kayleigh had texted her on the Saturday asking if she could stay another night with her friend. There was no cause for concern then.

Leicestershire CID were called in and later that Sunday afternoon they found Harlow, a sedentary university drop out aged twenty-seven, who spent most of his time in his grubby maisonette flat on the estate opposite Sence Valley Park. They asked him to come to the police station to help them and he did.

During the evening he told officers that Kayleigh had indeed stayed with him on Friday night and was with him on Saturday. He said he thought she was nineteen and that they had done sexual things together but not actually had sex.

His account continued that late on the Saturday afternoon he had wanted some mixers for his vodka. He went around to the flat which backed onto his and spoke to his neighbour Beadman, a self-employed landscape gardener and odd job man. Harlow and Beadman knew each other from their school days but were not particularly close friends.

He asked for some mixers but Beadman didn't have any so the lazy Harlow asked for a lift to the local Co-op, just over half a mile away. Beadman drove him there and they went into the Co-op together. Harlow then decided to get some more alcohol and he was asked for ID. Despite being overweight and out of shape, features that normally put years on a person, he had a bum fluff beard you would associate with a teenager. He had no ID, so Beadman took him to another smaller shop where he bought vodka and lemonade. Harlow then invited Beadman round to have a drink and meet his "*bird*".

According to Harlow they spent the night drinking together and Kayleigh got very drunk. About midnight he said he was off to bed and he left her with Beadman in his lounge, which was on the first floor above his ground floor bedroom. When he got up the next day neither Kayleigh nor Beadman were there and he was angry that Beadman had stolen Kayleigh from him.

He said that later that morning Beadman came to his place to pick some keys up. Beadman apparently told him that Kayleigh had gone.

Officers went to Beadman's flat but nobody was there. It was now getting late. The Leicestershire DI decided something was seriously wrong with all this. Not least because Kayleigh was still missing. The on-call EMSOU SIO was Martin in Lincolnshire. After a five minute version of the day's events, he told them to find Beadman and arrest him on suspicion of kidnap and do the same with Harlow, who was still in a police station anyway.

Beadman was found at his sister's house in the nearby town of Coalville. Martin started making his way to Beaumont Leys and by seven on Monday quite a few of us were assembled there. Initially Martin was set to run the job as SIO but mid-morning Kate was told by the Chief Officer with overall command of EMSOU that she would be running it. This was a missing teenager and unless we resolved it quickly and happily it would be a massive political and media hot potato.

There were about six DIs on the job initially. Martin stayed at Beaumont as the nominal deputy but I made sure he knew that it was a job I wanted as soon as he went back to Lincolnshire.

For now, different areas of responsibility were being handed out to the DIs. I knew which I wanted. I was brought up in North West Leicestershire and went to the same school, in Ashby-de-la-Zouch, that Kayleigh now attended. I wanted to be with the search and local investigation teams. I knew Ibstock better than any of the others, plus I liked to be out and about more than the average DI.

By the time I got to Ibstock the first Tactical Support Group (TSG) officers had started to arrive and so had two Nottinghamshire detectives. The base for the search was the car park for Sence Valley Forest Park.

The park is a sixty hectare area with three big lakes and a mass of woodland, mainly pine, larch and poplars. These wooded areas are thick in parts but in others you can easily walk about through the trees.

The first hypothesis was that Kayleigh had gone missing, probably at the hands of Harlow and/or Beadman and the starting point was where her phone had been found, on the road in between the estate they lived on and the park. Immediately adjacent to the place the phone had lain, was a footpath leading into the park. If you used that path you could get into the park twenty-four hours a day. About 150 yards up the road was the car park entrance which was locked at night.

The car park curves back round almost parallel to the road but with a few houses with big gardens in between the two. There is a children's nursery, a toilet block and a little information hut there. There was also a couple of large piles of gravel, presumably waiting to be used and a small fenced off area about the size of a tennis court that was very overgrown.

One of the Notts detectives was a DS called Cumbo. I had got to know him on the Wood Hill job when we realised we had been on the same initial training course in Warwickshire in 1987.

Cumbo is what people call a character. He was an old school detective. You could ask him to get any job done and it would *get* done. For example, after the fire we realised that a young Leicester City player, one who had played a few first team games, had met with one of the suspects much earlier on the day of the fire. We needed a detailed statement of what was said between them.

I made the mistake of sending the Power, a Leicester City season ticket holder, to see the player. He came back with four lines of rubbish, an autograph and a funny story about them beating Leeds in the League Cup. Yeah, I laughed too.

To sort it out I sent Cumbo back and the first thing he did was speak to Nigel Pearson, the big and fairly imposing manager of Leicester and a man of Cumbo's generation. Pearson told Cumbo that the lad would be co-operating fully and if there was the slightest suggestion of reluctance he wanted to know. Ten pages later we had the full account.

Cumbo was also hilarious and the master of the one liner. Once, I bumped into him coming out of a court room in Nottingham, shaking his head. I asked him what was up.

'*That fucking defence barrister in there*', he said, pointing over his shoulder.

'*He's a fucking cock. I've just said to him, oi pal, you're clutching at more straws than a scarecrow having a wank.*'

Anyway, back to Ibstock in 2015, Cumbo and his colleague had something to show me. They had found a bra. They had actually been tipped off to it by a call to the incident room. A dog walker had seen it on top of the vegetation in the fenced off area and linked it to the news item she had heard about a missing teenager.

The bra, in incongruously good condition for the surroundings, sat on top of the bushes and branches in the fenced off area. It had not been there long. I had it photographed and recovered and the Family Liaison Officers, Vinny and Alka, had the dubious honour of showing it to Stephanie. As it was bagged up, we noted the brand and the size.

Before long, the worst of news came back from the FLOs. The bra was the same make, size and colour as one of Kayleigh's. One that was not at her home.

I met up with the inspector in charge of the TSG. He was called Paul and he had graduated from being the best sergeant they had, to running the department. He was the best person I could possibly have hoped to be there.

Organised searches usually have one nationally accredited Police Search Advisor (PolSa) as the point person. The PolSa for this mammoth task was an ex-squaddie called Steve. It was his first major deployment since qualifying in the specialism. What a baptism of fire.

As well as Paul, the most experienced PolSa in the region, Steve had his own sergeant with him, Emma. She was another PolSa and someone else I liked and got on with. Then he had me breathing down his neck and always likely to be throwing him a curve ball and asking him to send his teams in another direction based on intelligence and information I was receiving.

He was the most supervised man in the world and he was going to have plenty to do.

Back at Beaumont, the interview teams were starting to get stuck into Beadman and Harlow. In television dramas the police interviewer is usually the Detective Superintendent or maybe a DI, like me. In reality, the bosses do not interview prisoners for serious offences. We would cock it up.

DCs and occasionally DSs, trained in advanced interview techniques and supervised by another detective, usually a DS who is an accredited interview advisor; they run the interviews.

On the occasions when I was at the station during interviews on jobs I was running, I was quite intrusive and a bit of a pain in the arse. I would always be looking for updates and putting new requirements into the advisor but I knew full well that they had a better chance of getting a result than I did.

Beadman was being interviewed by two of my own team: Karen, who had been Dr Taufiq's FLO and Steve. Harlow was dealt with by Eleanor, another of my team and Rob, a ginger Forest fan new to one of the other Leicestershire syndicates. All four of them did a fantastic job.

It is worth mentioning that the entire Leicestershire arm of EMSOU-Major Crime was on this job for the first three or four days. That's three DIs, five DSs, about twenty-five DCs and something to the order of fifteen support staff. A significant proportion of the teams from Nottingham, Derby, Lincolnshire and Northants were also sent over. This was what we called a *big job* even though in the grand scheme of things it did not turn out to be one of the more difficult ones to solve.

Karen and Steve knew that the most important thing they had to establish was where Kayleigh was. There are interview manuals and tactical guides and they are all very well but all we wanted to know was '*is Kayleigh alive and where is she?*'

Karen asked Beadman directly, right at the start of the interview, where Kayleigh was:

'We don't know where Kayleigh is. We don't know if she's alive or if she's not alive.' Beadman said he didn't know. He was deadpan. He said he had met her once at Harlow's and she was drunk. He had not seen her since.

Harlow, now in interview as a suspect rather than a witness, was pretty much sticking to his story, including that he thought Kayleigh was nineteen. Beadman was in tune with him up to midnight on Saturday. At that juncture Beadman said he went home, leaving Kayleigh with Harlow and he hadn't seen her since.

The standout thing about Beadman was that he had three fresh looking injuries to his face. They were red and had been bleeding. One was on his forehead above his left eye, one on his nose and one on his chin.

In a large investigation like this, information comes into a police incident room in many forms. Sometimes generated by the media releases the local force puts out. Sometimes from the hard work being done by police officers and staff working on it. This information can be witness statements from people like the builder who found Kayleigh's phone; calls to the police about possible sightings or about things they have seen on TV; reports from officers who have been given actions to complete; and intelligence developed and analysed by a department specialising in that important area of police work.

This all leads to a mountain of incoming data and the difficulty is in identifying which pieces are the most important. In a murder investigation each item is usually seen first by someone in the role of 'Receiver'. Leicestershire have had and still do have, some of the best of these.

The two there now in 2021 are both called Kev, they are both retired Detective Sergeants and both are outstanding at the job. I'm sure I could make a cheap crack about one of them having been around since Noah was a lad but I won't stoop to it. Also, he's much bigger than me.

The job entails the Receiver making a quick decision on whether an item needs some high priority work allocating from it immediately or whether it can wait. Sometimes the person submitting that information has worked out for themselves that it is important and got things moving. Sometimes they have not and the Receiver brings it to the attention of the SIO.

If important lines of enquiry slip through the net, it can be disastrous for an investigation and of course the Receivers, being human, can't be expected to remember every detail. This is where *HOLMES comes in*. The '*Home Office Large Major Enquiry System*' was developed after the Yorkshire Ripper enquiry in the 1980s. Then, a huge amount of information about Peter Sutcliffe had entered the incident room and nobody, apart from one ignored DC called Andrew Laptew, managed to join the dots.

In fact, computers *were* used on that investigation to trace vehicles seen in red light areas and to identify vehicles that could have left certain tyre tracks. Had both been persevered with, *both* would have led to a small and manageable set of results that included the cars Sutcliffe had been driving at relevant times. Unfortunately, the senior officers involved shut down these systems part way through. So, it was only after the enquiry into the failures of the investigation that *HOLMES* came about.

HOLMES is used by all forces in England and Wales. If it had been in use in 1984, every one of the multiple mentions of Sutcliffe would have raised a flag, each one in turn raising more and more suspicions. Good operators like the Kevs' and Leicestershire's best and most experienced HOLMES manager Sam and her team are still needed to make it a success. Over the many years that I used HOLMES, I just assumed that if I missed something Sam would tell me and I'd be able sort it out. And she did. On the TV, Lewis or Vera or whoever the SIO is solves the mystery on his or her own. In real life it does not work like that. With apologies to the makers of those programmes. I am sure they are great to watch.

One of the pieces of information to come in on that first day was a statement from someone who saw Beadman on Sunday afternoon, before the police had his name. This witness had asked him how he had got the injuries to his face and Beadman had said he fell over on Saturday morning, while doing some groundwork in a field for a farmer. The Receiver saw this, recognised it as important and made sure it reached the interview teams promptly.

Back in Ibstock, search officers flooded into what we came to call our search village during Monday and Tuesday. We had a collection of vans for the teams, a command van and mess facilities including a huge inflatable tent, all covering half of the car park. I went to the children's nursery and explained to the manager what was happening. She kindly agreed to close and started calling parents to collect the children.

The searchers were sent out in teams with specific sectors of the park to search, all worked out by Steve the PolSa. At the peak we estimated we had 400 officers deployed from about eight different police forces. This included helicopter and fixed wing support, specialist search dogs and deep water experts.

Before long, the bra and the phone were not the only indications that Sence Valley should be the focus of the search. On the footpath leading from where the phone had been seen, into the park, a searcher almost immediately spotted some material, fresh in appearance, sitting in the hedge bottom. It was the same type of material as the bra and it was the same colour.

On Tuesday morning we got intelligence from the incident room that Beadman was supposed to have a lock up somewhere. Two possible locations were given. This was urgent stuff. One was quickly ruled out but an account for a lock up in his name was found at a site in Diseworth, near to East Midlands Airport. A team raced up there and got the owner to open Beadman's lock up. It was outstandingly clean and tidy. Full of gardening equipment but there was nothing to do with Kayleigh in there.

The search team then set about looking at all the areas of the lock up site to which any renter could gain access. Just outside the main yard was a skip and inside that, on top of all the other rubbish, which was bagged up, were a jumper and a handbag. As with the bra they were photographed and recovered for forensic examination. The FLOs were given the same task to do and the same terrible result came back. They were Kayleigh's or at the very least identical to items she owned and which were currently missing.

The net was closing in on Beadman. He had been asked about his injuries and when he gave the same story about falling over in a field on Saturday, he was shown some CCTV that had just come in.

The images were of him and Harlow going into the Co-op on Saturday night, just as they said they had. As they left Beadman could be seen wearing a rugby shirt in similar green, white and red colours to a Leicester Tigers top. His face was in full view and he had no injuries.

Karen asked him about this and he said he had mixed his days up. It was Sunday morning that he fell over. The witness statement highlighted by the Receiver was then discussed. He said the witness was wrong. He still insisted he had not seen Kayleigh since he had left Harlow's flat.

The specialist advisor supervising the interviewers was in fact the younger of the aforementioned two Kevs, who was still a serving officer at the time. He was my team sergeant for long periods and he was reliability on legs. He deserves as much credit as any of the interviewers for the methodical destruction of Beadman and Harlow's stories. He passed through the location to us in Ibstock, where Beadman said he had been working when he fell. It was a field owned by a local farmer near the village of Belton.

I sent Cumbo and his DC on ahead and then followed with the TSG. By the time we got there the Notts pair had made the key discovery themselves. In the field were some rickety put up buildings, various piles of rubble and general farmyard detritus plus, incongruously, a Shetland Pony. At the back of the field was a prepared bonfire, waiting to be lit. At the bottom of this was a bin liner and with a gentle pull with a stick to open it they could see it appeared to contain bloodstained clothing. The bag was carefully emptied by the search team and one item in particular stood out. It was a rugby shirt, in green, red and white. And it was heavily bloodstained.

Over the next twenty-four hours Karen and Steve started turning the screws on Beadman. His next problem was that three witnesses driving up the A447 about 10am on Sunday morning had seen a man walking towards Ibstock, on the opposite side of the road to Sence

Valley Park. All three of these people said the man they saw was using a mobile phone and had noticeable cuts to his face.

Beadman denied that this was him.

More statements began to come in. People living in one of the flats that adjoined Harlow's heard banging and crashing about, around 10pm that night. A lady living on an adjacent street heard screaming and shouting coming from the direction of Harlow's flat at 3am.

A man living on another new estate, which was opposite Harlow and Beadman's and adjacent to the footpath into Sence Valley, had also heard something significant. He was in bed with his partner around 3.30am when he got up because he couldn't sleep. He opened a window to get some fresh air.

As he did this, he was sure he heard the voice of a girl shout '*Mummy, Mummy!*'. He was so certain that he went straight outside for a cigarette and stood in the garden listening. When he heard nothing else, he went back to bed.

We also had one eyewitness. A man living in a house on Harlow and Beadman's estate heard a commotion outside and looked out of his bedroom window. He lived near to the road and had a view of a footpath that ran from beyond Harlow's to the A447 and he could just see the entrance to the Sence Valley Park path, where the fragment of bra material had been found.

What he *thought* he saw when he looked down from his first floor window was a police officer detaining someone on the ground. Then he realised that the man was not a policeman, just someone wearing a jacket with a reflective stripe on the back.

He thought about going outside to intervene or calling the police but as he watched them the man and the other person, who he could now see was a girl, walked away together into the estate. He noticed that the girl appeared to be wearing little, if anything, on her lower half.

A few minutes later he heard another noise and looked out once more. This time he saw the same two people walking back in the other direction. He felt sure that one said to the other '*Hold my hand.*' He saw them cross the road towards the footpath into Sence Valley Park.

Aside from her killer, he was the last person to see Kayleigh Haywood alive.

I was certain that the walking man witnessed by three passing motorists on Sunday morning was Beadman. My worry though was not *who* he was but *where* he was. All our efforts were concentrated on searching Sence Valley Forest Park. This man, if it *was* Beadman, was on the opposite side of the road from the park, walking towards it, not away from or out of it.

On the morning of Wednesday 18th November, I attended the usual briefing in which everyone was updated on the various arms of the investigation. This included the three witness sightings of the bleeding man on his phone.

A couple of hours later I was sitting in a van in the search village enjoying a sausage cob, which I had of course covered liberally in brown sauce. (Leicestershire word alert: a sausage cob is a bread roll with a sausage in it).

It is worth mentioning that the cob was delivered free of charge by a group of scouts. The community spirit and the will to find Kayleigh was amazing. People all over Ibstock and Measham plus many more from miles around, turned up regularly, asking what they could do to help. Locals took to putting up purple ribbons everywhere as a symbol of hope for Kayleigh.

Everyone wanted the best possible outcome but that morning the boss, Kate, had just made the only decision she could. We all thought that Kayleigh was dead now and on her instructions the interviewers arrested Beadman and Harlow on suspicion of murder. This dropped a feeling of dread and gloom over the village like a huge blanket, suffocating the hope out of friends, relatives and strangers alike.

Sitting in the van, in between mouthfuls of cob, I answered my phone to a Derbyshire EMSOU detective and was invited to meet her and her crew mate on the A447, not far from where the bleeding man had been seen walking.

I walked down with two TSG officers and saw the Derby cops. They pointed me to a ditch on the opposite side of the road. I could see some screwed up clothing in the bottom. It looked like it had been there for a while but we could all clearly see that one of the items was denim and Kayleigh had been wearing a sleeveless denim top when she left home on Friday. It was a great piece of intuition on their part. It would have been a couple of days before our search plan reached that area. The Derby detectives had been paying attention at the briefing and decided to check the area out.

We recovered the clothing and I took it back to Beaumont to hand to our exhibits officer. The FLOs were in the office; Vinny and Alka did a fantastic job throughout this. As soon as they saw the denim top through the window in the exhibit bag, they both knew it was Kayleigh's top.

The thing with searching is that you can't do it effectively in the dark. I got back to Beaumont for the second time around 5pm on the Wednesday afternoon. We had stood the teams down. The TSG inspector, Paul, was with me for the late briefing but we never got to go to it.

Karen and Steve had just interviewed Beadman for the umpteenth time. At the end of the interview, he said he wanted a private word with his appropriate adult. People have asked me why he had one of those and I can't remember but the Custody Sergeant must have read something into the answers to his routine questions that merited it. Some vulnerability that meant he should have an extra person, as well as his solicitor, to advise him on what to do.

I read something on LinkedIn recently, about a police officer dealing with a prisoner who didn't have a solicitor. In the case described, the officer made sure the prisoner spoke to a solicitor for his own protection, even though the prisoner had not asked for one.

You would think, from the crap that followed in the LinkedIn message thread, that this was a noble and rare act. In reality, we often made sure that it was a fair fight by doing that, either with a solicitor or an appropriate adult. One defence solicitor commenting on the LinkedIn post nailed it: We did not want to leave the defendant with an appeal point or some get out clause later on because he didn't receive the proper advice and support. It is basics.

Anyway, back to the job. Beadman wanted to speak to his appropriate adult. Steve was in the room when he made the request. Karen and Beadman's solicitor had both taken a break.

Steve stepped outside and waited but after about ten minutes the appropriate adult called him back in and told Steve he could no longer represent Beadman and we needed to replace him.

Beadman had coughed the job to him. He had told the appropriate adult that he knew where Kayleigh was and that she was dead. Steve quickly raised the alarm and after a short time another person was found to support Beadman and the interview resumed.

I spoke to Kate and with her approval, Paul and I went straight back to Ibstock.

Karen and Steve were told; *one objective, find out where Kayleigh is.*

As soon as we arrived in Ibstock, we got the first update. Beadman was talking to them. Kayleigh was not in Sence Valley Forest Park. According to him she was in fields on the opposite side of the road. He was saying the location was a good way into those fields and in deep undergrowth, in a hedge.

It was pitch black and raining heavily. Paul and I started walking diagonally into the fields away from the direction of Sence Valley. After about half a mile we came to some kind of a track overgrown with bushes and brambles. We could see on a phone mapping app that it was a discontinued rail track called the Blackberry Line. It looked as though there was still a bridge on the line, about 200 metres over to our right, which dissected a large pond. We headed that way.

Paul made a call and we arranged for Steve and Karen to get Beadman to mark on a map where he thought Kayleigh was. This was then compared to the tracking signal in Paul's airwave radio. While we waited for them to get back to us, we walked onto the bridge. Paul's phone rang and as he answered it, I followed him.

At one point I saw him step to the side and his free hand briefly flicked out and pointed down. About a second before I would have fallen forty feet to my death, I saw that he was pointing to a massive hole under which was nothing and then just black water.

'What the fuck was that?!' I said, 'The international hand signal for watch out there's a great big hole and you might die?'

He just looked at me and I heard him say something about detectives and shake his head.

For about an hour we tried to figure out where Steve and Karen were directing us but it became clear that the map they were using was not how the field looked in the present. We had decent torches and dragon lights but they were starting to fade.

At one point someone decided to send X-Ray 55, the air support unit, overhead. It was immediately clear that the glare of their spotlights just made things worse on the canopy of trees we were in and around. I should have told them to leave straight away but we let them have a good look. Was there still some part of me thinking, 'what if she's still alive? Maybe their thermal imaging cameras will pick up her body heat?' I don't think that's the case but perhaps, subconsciously, it crossed my mind.

Sometime between 8pm and 9pm we were joined by Emma and Steve. They had fresh torches. By now we were being told that Beadman was claiming that Kayleigh had hit him with a brick and he had then thrown it at her head, killing her.

By 9.45pm we had found nothing. The four of us moved into a group to speak. It was chucking it down with rain, it was dark and cold. We agreed that there was no point recalling the search teams until it was light the next day. But we also agreed that we four, could not stop. We needed to carry on regardless.

I recalled that a few hundred yards away we had skirted the edge of a new building site being prepared. I wondered whether Kayleigh might be there, given that a brick had been mentioned. I suggested we go and look but I deferred to Paul. This was his world.

Paul favoured going back to a spot we had looked at earlier, about fifty yards from the location Beadman had given the interviewers. There was a small v shape of grass into some dense undergrowth there and before Emma and Steve had arrived, we had gone a few yards into it but stopped because it was so overgrown. It was not that we couldn't get through it, more that we thought no one else had got through before us. We headed back there, at one point walking through some really wet, boggy ground to the side of the pond. Then when we got to the v we spread out a bit and started forcing our way through.

Paul and I were towards the front, Steve and Emma a bit farther back. Steve was to the left of the rest of us. Once through the first thirty or forty yards it opened up a bit and a vague path was discernible, albeit still overgrown.

At 10,10pm Steve suddenly shouted, '*Got her!*'

We all made our way over to him. He had crested the rise of a small bank and there lay the still form of a young white girl with fair hair. She was naked except for one sock and she was in an odd, twisted position, partly on her front and partly on her side. Her face was a mess. She had been gravely injured by someone or something.

While we were doing this, Kate and Martin the Lincs DCI along with Vinny and Alka, had gone over to Measham to see Kayleigh's mum and dad. I think they spoke to the family and then went and sat nearby in their cars. Two or three times Martin called me to ask me if we had found anything and by the last call I was getting a bit fed up with it, telling him he would be the first person I contacted if we did.

Now it was time for that call. Martin thanked me and they went back into the Haywood home and Kate told them what we had found. It was heart-breaking. All four detectives there were parents. All four were feeling it.

Passing on news like that is something that comes your way as a cop on a regular basis. Nobody likes to have to break tragic news over the phone in the way Matt had to with Dr Taufiq. In person is better but it is still terrible. There is no question in my mind which is the worst job and that night my four colleagues in Measham had it; not Paul, Steve, Emma and I, who stood by Kayleigh's body, hating every fibre of Beadman and wishing it could have been different.

As a homicide investigator you can never give the victim's loved ones what they want. You can never bring that person back from the dead. What you see is real human pain. It is horrendous and it does take its toll on people. Personally, I felt the need to keep my emotions in check. I was there to do a job. This was not happening to me and I would not have to live with that loss afterwards. It felt fraudulent to even compare my feelings to theirs.

One of my worst memories is not from a homicide but a tragic accident. A man had been showing his baby daughter the view from his HGV when she slipped from his grasp. She fell to the ground outside, cracking her head on the metal step as she went. She died shortly after the deployed air ambulance got her to hospital. I was sent out to investigate it and to make sure it was as innocent as it sounded and of course it was. It was just a proud dad with his little girl but what I saw there was raw grief and I have never forgotten it. Bad as it was for me though, it was a million times worse for that poor man and his wife. My heart bled for them.

Getting back to Kayleigh, I arranged for some uniform night shift officers to meet us on the A447. Paul and I had probably walked around four miles that night but by the quickest route, over a ploughed field, across the Blackberry Line, through a grassed field, around the lake and into the undergrowth at the v, to where Kayleigh was, was probably about a half to three quarters of a mile. You could not get a road vehicle any closer.

I assured Martin that he could tell Kayleigh's parents that she would not be left alone at any point and using a few officers we formed as good a cordon as we could in the dark. We had seen a spent shotgun cartridge on the ground in the thicket so it wasn't impossible that a poacher or dog walker would come ambling through. The four of us then went back to Beaumont. I arranged to meet Barbara the Senior CSI in Ibstock the next day and went home for three or four hours sleep.

At 8am the next morning, it had stopped raining and we got a TSG van down a track to the closest point, along with the CSI vans used by Barbara and Ken (yes them again) and a couple of other CSIs. I guided them over to the site and in through the cordon so that they could start the long and painstaking job of harvesting the evidence; much of which would come from the careful, forensic recovery of Kayleigh's body.

The scene was so different in the light. The lack of rain helped. Less than ten metres from Kayleigh's body was a fast flowing stream, below a steep bank. The previous night none of us had any idea it was there. I also realised that the boggy ground we had walked through in the dark was part of the pond. Later I wondered how Kayleigh must have felt at 4am with her killer. I wondered if she knew what was going to happen. I'd like five minutes with him but then I guess I'm in a long queue.

Needless to say, the media were on to us in a flash. At one stage I went out into the grassed field where Ken was setting up a 3D video to film the surroundings and potential routes Beadman and Kayleigh could have taken. There were quite a few journalists and photographers approaching through the field, although an officer made sure they didn't get too close to the v. A couple of camera crews had also made the trek.

Suddenly, from nowhere a man appeared and it seemed he was the farmer. I got to know him a bit better later. He was called Pete.

In classic style he actually shouted, '*Ger off my fuckin' land!*' at them all.

It was the farmland equivalent of hearing someone at a garden party say, '*More tea vicar?*'

I went over for a word and we established that we were both old Ashby Grammar School boys - this being the place, now called just Ashby School, that Kayleigh had also attended. He told me he didn't want the bastards on his land. I defended them a little bit. I had used the media a lot in investigations, sometimes, such as on the Dogan Dogan job, to great effect.

I said, '*They're only doing their job Pete, they won't get in our way.*'

He said OK and he indicated them to move back. He signalled to a few of them that they would get a better view from the bridge above the pond.

I said, '*I think I was up there last night. There's a big hole in it you know.*'

He looked at me to see if I really thought this was news to him and said, '*I know. It's been condemned for a few years now. I must get round to putting a new sign up*'

As far as I know, no members of the fourth estate went missing that day.

The next problem was that a helicopter appeared and from news that I was told was starting to appear on TV, we worked out that it was from Sky. Barbara was getting to the point where she had done all she could do with Kayleigh's body. Soon she would want us to move her but she needed about twenty minutes in a space where she could tell there was a view through the trees from above. We did not want pictures of Kayleigh's uncovered body on the TV. Barbara asked me if I could get rid of the helicopter for half an hour.

I made two calls. One to Matt Tapp, the Leicestershire Police Communications Director. I had met him a few times and got to know him a little bit. That was to become a friendship and lead to us working together more later. For now, I wondered if he knew anyone at Sky who he could ask to get rid of the chopper.

The force control room inspector was Ivan again and I called him too. This is the same Ivan who was laughing at my predicament on my stag do in 1992. He seemed to be around at a lot of important times when I was on a job. He and I go way back. He is one of these ridiculously naturally fit people, like Spradders, who can be sedentary for weeks and then go out and run a half marathon for a laugh like Seb Coe. Irritating.

I said to Ivan I didn't care if he called the East Midlands Airport Control Tower or whistled up a pair of Tornados to shoot it down but could he *please get rid of that bloody helicopter*.

I don't know which of them succeeded first (they both claimed the credit) but ten minutes later the chopper cleared off. Twenty minutes after that Barbara said we could take Kayleigh. I gathered together the nine or ten TSG officers and told them we would have to carry her the half mile or so over fields and I wanted them to do it without ever putting her on the ground.

I had perhaps quite naively tried to persuade the assembled media not to film when we brought her out. One of them said that his editor would kill him if everyone else got the pictures and he didn't. It was a poor choice of words.

Of course, there *was* news footage and there were many photos but I can say that the ladies and gentlemen of the Leicestershire TSG were magnificent. Kayleigh was in a black body bag on a bright orange stretcher and they carried her, with the occasional slick changeover of bearers, the whole way to the waiting undertakers van, without stopping and without the stretcher being put down on the ground.

Back in the interview room Karen and Steve had got stuck into Beadman again. He now admitted that it was him the witness had seen pinning Kayleigh down outside his house. She had run from

Harlow's flat with nothing on her lower half, not wanting to be with them anymore.

Karen asked him if he had forced Kayleigh to walk across the road to the park and he agreed that he had. He also admitted that on the gravel of the car park there, he had raped her. The bastard.

This is where the sheer professional restraint of the experienced detective comes in. Everything in the fibre and being of Karen and Steve was telling them that they should wring the neck of this creature but they did not. They could not. They had to continue gaining his trust and persuading him to speak.

Beadman said they then went on a bit of a convoluted walk out of Sence Valley, down the road and across into the fields on the opposite side of the road. He apparently knew the land because it backed onto to a garden centre in the village of Ellistown, where he had once worked.

Once they got well into the fields, he said Kayleigh suddenly pushed him over and ran off, down the slope towards the pond. He caught her up and as he did so she '*chomped*' him in the face with a brick. His word.

She did this two or three times, he said, so he grabbed the brick and threw it hard at her head, killing her. After that he claimed he left her in some bushes and went home.

The last part was absolute horse shit and we were about to prove it.

To take the investigation forward Kate made me the official Deputy SIO and we selected a DC called Andy to be the OIC. We had already worked out that the grooming angle would be significant and that we would need to look at the media profiles and electronic devices of Beadman and Harlow in detail. Kayleigh might not be their only victim.

Andy was the office geek. He even had a mug with that written on it. He knew more about social media, phones, computers and tablets than anyone else in the department. Added to which it was time he had a big job and he was as keen as mustard.

Over the course of the next few months Andy did a fantastic job. He downloaded over 2,600 messages exchanged between Harlow and Kayleigh in the two weeks before she met him and stayed at his house. They were, in the typical style of the loathsome groomer he was, often flesh crawlingly complimentary. Some made references to him wanting to kidnap Kayleigh. These were particularly disturbing.

Andy had also managed to get some key messages to Rob and Eleanor while Harlow was still being interviewed. It was quite clear from them that he knew full well she was fifteen. In one particularly good session which I didn't see until it was used in a TV documentary months later, Rob, to coin a line from Monty Python amongst others, *took him to the fucking cleaners.*

He painstakingly led Harlow through his despicable behaviour and made him admit each and every disgusting aspect of it. Rob spoke in almost a whisper, asking the squirming Harlow to justify his actions. Of course, he couldn't. It was great work.

Beadman was charged with rape and murder. Harlow was charged with grooming Kayleigh and sexually assaulting her.

A few weeks later we met our barristers, Miranda, the QC and Teresa, her number two. They were both outstanding. By the time we had our first meeting with them I had some results from a separate line of enquiry I had set up.

The Grooming Team as I called them, consisted of a syndicate of Major Crime detectives under the command of their efficient DS, Paula. This group, which included our FLO Alka, did me a brilliant job. They dissected the social media accounts of Harlow looking for evidence of other girls he had groomed or tried to groom.

Beadman, it turned out, didn't really have a social media presence but Andy then made another chilling discovery. We knew that Beadman had been out and about and had visited his lock-up in Diseworth. We had CCTV of him sitting in his car there plus we had found Kayleigh's jumper and bag in the skip. What we *didn't* really know was what he had been planning to do next.

Andy was able to shed some light on it. In between Kayleigh's death and his arrest Beadman had been searching for lime pits on the internet. Who does that? He was planning to get rid of the evidence in the most gruesome way.

At the meeting with counsel, we were able to put four or five potential new cases of grooming by Harlow up for consideration. I won't describe any in great detail, I don't want the oik trying to sue me so I'll just say that Miranda and Teresa felt there were two more cases in which the evidence was overwhelming.

Where Miranda and Teresa really impressed me though was when we discussed false imprisonment as a new charge for both defendants. Andy had shown that Kayleigh had stopped using her phone about 9pm on Saturday night. This was unheard of for her. Witnesses then heard and saw significant things as already described in these pages.

Crucially, one of those witnesses talked about a young girl with no clothing on the lower half of her body. She had run from the house like that. This was compelling as far as our female barristers were concerned and it would be compelling to a jury.

Miranda said we should charge them both with false imprisonment. The CPS would have you believe they make the decisions at this juncture. They certainly do when the police have prisoners in custody but once counsel are appointed, the CPS just do what they are told. So do the police.

Beadman pleaded guilty to rape and murder pretty much as soon as he could. Harlow went guilty to grooming, sexual assault and one of the two new grooming charges. He decided to brazen it out on the other one. They both said they were not guilty of false imprisonment.

Some people asked the very valid question: Why are you going ahead with a trial for false imprisonment? What difference does it make? Why put the parents through it?

These were all good questions but we had another purpose. On the narrow point of false imprisonment, we were able to tell the whole story. We were also able to smash apart Beadman's bullshit story about being hit with a brick and retaliating, causing Kayleigh's death.

Kayleigh had multiple injuries to the back of her head and multiple injuries to her face including a fractured jaw. She also had classic defence injuries to her hand. He had subjected her to an horrific beating.

A Home Office pathologist examined photos of Beadman with *his* injuries and expressed an expert written opinion that he had *not* sustained them by being hit in the face with a brick. Apart from anything else he wore glasses and these were fine. The pathologist was of the view that Beadman had hurt himself in a fall onto uneven ground.

On the first day of the trial, when Harlow realised we were going to produce his second extra grooming victim as a live witness, he changed his plea to guilty on this offence too.

During the trial, for the most part the cowardly Beadman stayed in the cells. He came up when Harlow gave evidence and spent the whole time tutting and shaking his head. In that evidence Harlow was systematically taken apart by Miranda. He was made to look like the grubby sexual deviant he is.

Both were convicted of all offences and crucially Harlow got an extra seven years for the false imprisonment charge. Twelve years in total. Some vindication that. He will be out soon though. Presumably, he will have the sense not to come back to Leicestershire.

Beadman was sentenced to life with a minimum term to serve of thirty-five years. Many months later, in a TV documentary about the case I was asked why I thought Beadman had done it. Why had he inflicted this barbaric assault on Kayleigh?

'*Probably because he could*' I said, 'Probably *because he could.*'

In April 2021 Stephen Beadman died in prison.

Matt Tapp, who as I have said, became a friend, had an idea about turning Kayleigh's story into an educational film. He had sat and read all the messages between Harlow and Kayleigh.

With the support of her parents this was achieved and the film, *Kayleigh's Love Story* was given the green light. Matt contacted a firm called *Affixxius* in Loughborough and they produced an amazing product. I was a technical advisor on some of the content but a minor player really. The credit goes to Matt who had been a communications and media expert, working for many different forces for donkeys' years.

The film was a re-telling of the story of Kayleigh falling for the despicable Harlow and then paying the gravest of penalties. A number of us ended up involved in the initial screenings in community and educational venues across Leicestershire.

The film has now been seen by tens of millions of children all around the world. If one life has been saved, then Matt Tapp and Affixxius in particular, deserve the credit.

Bath 2016

AFTER ALL that, the golf trip was a bit flat for me. We did the races again which was a laugh but personally the golf was as bad it could be for me. Added to which the take up was the smallest since the first trip to Whitby in 1998. Only sixteen signed up.

I scored ten points. A joke of a total. I just could not hit the golf ball and the harder I tried the worse it got. Gordon would have had a fighting chance against me, albeit he would still have needed a personal best.

Afterwards, we went for a meal in Bath. This was actually the part I enjoyed the most. I sat with Jason, Darren and Matt. We had some good food, good conversation and with Matt in the chair, some delicious red wine.

Matt is someone I haven't mentioned in detail in these pages apart from him deciding to save a few quid by booking us into a shit version of Fawlty Towers for my stag do.

We were crew mates back in the day, in uniform, at Braunstone Police Station. We had a good cop bad cop act that I have never been able to replicate with anyone else. Not too many people have ever been scared of me but in those days you would hurt yourself if you bumped into Matt and you really didn't want to fight him. Faced with having to deal with him, people would tell me almost anything.

On one night shift we were crewed up and we had a new officer in the back who was my sprog, as we called them. He was another

Simon. I was a tutor constable at the time and I was meant to be teaching him how to do things properly.

The shift was coming to a close about half six in the morning when the control room operator asked for a car to respond to a call on the Mowmacre Hill Estate near to Beaumont Leys Police Station. It wasn't on our patch but we volunteered to go. No-one else seemed bothered, probably more interested in getting home to bed.

A woman had called in and said she had come downstairs and caught her next door neighbour in her kitchen with a pair of her knickers in his hand. We had a chat with her. She was not at all traumatised and she surprised us when she said she didn't want him arresting. She said she would speak to his wife and tell her what he had been up to. That would ruin his entire year apparently. All our complainant wanted was for us to recover something. No, not the knickers.

She told us she had come home a couple of times recently to find things apparently moved in the house. She convinced herself it was her imagination but she was slightly niggled by the fact that she had lost a spare back door key. Now, having found this weirdo in her house, about to sniff her pants, everything was suddenly explained.

So, all this lady wanted was the back door key returning but she told us the weirdo wouldn't be at home. He would be at the local newsagent's getting his bags of newspapers sorted. She said he was such a waste of space that the only job he could hold down in his mid-forties was a paper round and he had four of them.

We found him right where we were told he would be, duly pointed out to us by the newsagent. He was a weaselly looking individual with long greasy dirty hair and a scruffy moustache. I asked him to come out to the car and we stood next to it.

I told him what we suspected him of and asked him to give me the key. He denied it all.

Oh, the outrage! How dare we?

Matt just snarled, '*Here we go. I'm not having this. I'm going to break his neck!*'

The pervert looked slightly alarmed and was staring at Matt.

I said, '*Don't look at him, you'll only make him worse. Let's get in the car.*'

We got in and Matt stayed outside. One of the windows was deliberately down. Simon was in the back, not in on the act, which is what it all was.

'*Look mate you need to give me the key*' I said.

'*I haven't got a key honestly*' he whined. At this Matt banged the bonnet of the car, making the man and Simon jump. I was ready for it.

'*For fucks sake!*' Matt shouted '*That's it! I'm having him. Shutts get of the car! Let me have the bastard. I can't stand perverts!*' He banged the car again and then started circling it menacingly, looking in at the man, whose head was now on a swivel.

The guy by now was shaking like a leaf.

I said, '*Look mate, you've seen him. I can't control him. Never mind you, he scares me. If he gets hold of you, you are fucking toast and I will not be getting in the way.*'

'*OK, OK,*' he stammered. '*Here's the key. Just keep him away from me at the police station. Ker ker keep him away.....you, you, per per promise?*'

I took the key, got out, walked around and opened his door.

'*What police station? You can go now*' I said.

He got out, still warily looking at Matt who was just staring at him. I explained:

'*Your neighbour doesn't want to press charges but think on...by the time you get home your missus will know about this and the knicker sniffing.*

I winked and smiled. '*Have a nice day.*'

We got back in the car and shook hands on a job well done. Simon just burst out laughing and said it was the best performance he had ever seen.

Back to Bath, I did have a slight resurgence in golfing terms during our friendly round on the Friday. Addo was a CID veteran who had never been on the trip before. He is a proper golfer and won the competition with thirty-five points, playing off a handicap of five.

On the Friday I partnered him against our very own Ant and Dec; Alan and Blackie.

As we teed off on the ninth, Addo and I were already three holes down. Alan and Blackie are good golfers and Addo was giving them both shots because of his low handicap. He needed a partner to kick in and help him. He had me. I was playing better than on my round of misery the day before but you can't polish a turd, as they say.

The ninth was a par three and the others all hit the green with their tee shots. I hit the bank next to it. As we walked forwards my phone rang and I realised it was a call I needed to take. By the time I had finished with that and got to my ball, I found it nestled in some nasty rough on a down slope about twenty five yards from the pin. I plucked my wedge and putter from the bag on our buggy. They had all putted out and were watching me.

Alan laughed, '*You won't need the putter son. You have got to get up and down in two to halve the hole and stay in the match.*'

I took the wedge and slashed at the ball which flew up in the air, bounced and rolled into the hole. We didn't halve the hole, we won it. Addo was ecstatic and for the rest of the match I played well; as did Addo.

On the eighteenth tee we were one up but we blew it and the match ended in a draw. Great fun.

It was a good end to a trip I had found underwhelming. Perhaps the trips had run their course after nineteen years.

2017 retirement and 2018 Bournemouth

2017 WAS a busy year for EMSOU Major Crime. It was also to be my last as a serving officer. I still had two more investigations as SIO though. In January, a lovely lady and mum of two, Kiran Daudia, was murdered by her estranged husband in Leicester. He crammed her body into a suitcase and tried to dispose of her amongst the wheelie bins of a house in a neighbouring street.

I also had the case of Timothy Smith, killed by two young men for no good reason. Tim took some chances with his personal life and one night in Shepshed in North Leicestershire he took one too many. He made an online arrangement to meet a man called Mark Law. Law turned up with his friend Mason Casey and stabbed Tim.

Law pleaded guilty but Casey tried his luck at trial. James, our junior barrister to Richard back in 2014 was by now a top QC and he was our guy. We had a good case against Casey but James was nothing short of brilliant against a very competent defence counsel.

There was no golf trip in 2017 and I was content to finish after nineteen outings but some of the boys let me know that they were not so happy with it. Jason and Greg were two of them and two people I have a lot of time for and so I agreed. The twentieth and last golf trip would take place in 2018. I would be a civilian by then but said I would do it.

I retired as a police officer on 27th October 2017 with thirty years and two days service. On 2nd December I went back to work for Matt Tapp and was involved in the project to make another internet safety film, *Breck's Last Game*, about the dangers of online gaming for young people.

I made a brief return to Major Crime work at the beginning of 2018 when I helped Wes, the DS who had been my deputy during the investigation of the Kiran Daudia murder, with the trial. Kiran's estranged husband was convicted. My last one.

In June 2018 we duly returned to Bournemouth. It couldn't really be anywhere else could it? It was a great trip, starting naturally in Hot Rocks in the sunshine. Addo came back and won it. Bingo tried his luck once more but I hadn't forgotten his words on his last outing. I gave him a single figure handicap and my pants stayed up. He didn't get near any prizes.

I would have loved Alan to take the final trophy but, rather prophetically, he scored twenty-two points, tying for eleventh with me.

And then

IN THE spring of 2019 Alan and I had a beer and decided we would go abroad on a little trip.

We decided eight was about the right number. In the event Matt couldn't make it and the Major didn't want to come so just six of us signed up.

Alan, Jamie, Lee, Baras, Blackie and I seemed like a good crowd of trip veterans. We picked Albufeira in Portugal and it was a great success. I booked us into a decent all-inclusive hotel. I shared a suite with Alan and Blackie and the others had an identical one.

We played a round on our first day at a decent course only ten minutes from the hotel. There was water on every hole. Hilarious for Blackie. Horrendous for me. Although, not just me as it turned out.

On a par three directly over water we saw Alan hit what looked like decent shot onto the green but then it seemed to roll back into the lake in front of it. We watched from a distance as he walked round to the green and then gave us a thumbs up. He could see his ball. He was going in.

It was like Jean Van-de-Velde at the 1999 Open, except that there was no Peter Alliss calling it '*pure madness*' this time. If anything, this was crazier as unlike the Frenchman, Alan *did* hit the ball from the water and we watched in amazement as he connected and it rocketed out of the lake.

Unfortunately for him it went about twenty-five yards, hit a massive tree and rebounded back over his head and into the lake again.

We played a wonderful championship course on the middle day and I even managed not to come last, which I had expected to do in this company. Blackie's coaching eked just enough points out of me to beat Jamie.

On day three we were back at the first course we had played. We had some fun on the tenth hole. As we arrived at the tee, a par three, there was a young woman sitting behind a table. All very smartly turned out and of course her English put us to shame. On the table was a selection of golfing treats, boxes of balls, caps, that sort of thing.

She announced to us that for ten euros we could enter a competition. The prize for a hole in one was tickets to the Ryder Cup. More realistically, the prize for landing a tee shot on the green was anything of your choice from the table. All the fun of the fair on a golf course in the Algarve.

It looked inviting but Baras and I were playing like complete dogs. We said no to her kind offer and explained that if she watched us tee off, she would understand. Lee decided to have a pop and handed over a ten euro note.

I went first and as if to prove my point, hit my ball under some bushes off to the right and way short of the green. Baras didn't do much better, largely because he was still laughing at my shot. Baras spends a lot of time laughing, which when you think about it is not a bad thing.

Lee then creamed one straight at the green. Baras and I said we would walk forward and confirm it. Sure enough it was on the green, fifteen feet from the pin. A great shot. We signalled back and saw the lady offering him the choice of the table.

After Baras and I had scuffed our balls forward we all met up to have a putt. Lee was holding a sleeve of three Srixon golf balls.

'Is that your prize?' said Baras.

'Yes' he said. *'I thought I was going to get the whole box.'*

'So, you've just paid ten euros to enter a competition to win nine euros worth of golf balls' I said.

'Yes'

Baras didn't say anything. He was on the floor laughing again.

On the last night we all went out for a few beers in Albufeira. While we were there, in a bar, I got a text from Katy. She informed me that she was at home with my old mate Ian's wife, Sally. They were settling down with the popcorn to watch *me* on TV. I had forgotten all about it: A TV documentary, covering a murder I had investigated, was being shown.

Before long, another text arrived. They apparently hadn't done me a favour with the actor playing me in the reconstruction. Apparently he was a short bloke with dyed hair. Charming.

Then I started getting shit from Ian himself, who was at home in Devon.

Text: *I thought you said John Travolta was playing you. Instead it's some fat chump wearing your white shirt.*

One of them sent me a picture of the actor which amused the boys no end. Then, as if on cue this little bloke walked into the bar wearing a white shirt, just like mine. They persuaded me to go and ask him for a selfie which fortunately he was too pissed and too bemused to complain about.

About 1am I decided I had drunk enough beer. My habit when drunk has often been just to decide to leave and walk off without telling anyone. It hasn't always gone to plan. I was told to get off a bus on one occasion in Leicester city centre when I tried to argue with the driver about his - I thought - mistaken intended destination. Another time, I got on the non-stop Leicester to London St Pancras train instead of the ten minute ride to the village where I lived. Nobody's perfect.

In Portugal, Alan was at pains to make sure I did not get lost. He said he had promised Katy he would look after me. So, when I stood up, he asked for volunteers to go with me. He was not so invested in my protection that he was going to stop drinking himself and he got away with that because Jamie took the chance to leave too and we headed back. Alan and Blackie woke me up at 5am when their keys apparently wouldn't work. I woke *them* up at 6.30 for the 7am taxi to the airport. Some things never change.

In the weird world that 2020 and 2021 have become I typed the last 40,000 words of this book for something to do while the world was in various stages of lockdown.

Alan and I are good friends these days and socialise with and without our better halves. He is retired too. I ended up as a Detective Inspector investigating murders while he made it to Detective Superintendent. No-one knows how. Only kidding mate.

Ian, who I went out with on my first day on patrol a lifetime ago, now lives in Devon. We still enjoy many a beer together, our families are close friends and he is God Father to both of my children. He retired in the same year as me and now holds the impressive record of having worked for three emergency services: police, ambulance and coast guard. He doesn't shout quite so much now.

And the unique Eddie remains the best jailer in the busiest custody suite in Leicester. He has moved out to a small village in the east of the county and last I heard was thinking of standing for mayor. The fact that they don't currently have a mayor is unlikely to stop him.

As for me, I have investigated my last murder. I retired from the force having done my thirty years at the end of 2017 and have dabbled with a few things since then including working as an investigator and trainer.

Maybe, when the world returns to normal, I will be able to arrange another jaunt to Portugal to soak up the sun and hit a few more balls.

As for the full version of the *golf trip* and visits to places like Blackpool, Brighton, Bath and Bournemouth; I'm afraid those days are over.

Probably.

Acknowledgements

Thanks to everyone who has answered a question or confirmed a fact for me. You know who you are. Gary gets a special mention for reminding me of some important details about the Russell case.

Thanks to Stephanie & Martin for giving me your blessing to talk about Kayleigh. I know it still hurts.

Thanks to Matt T & Dave (*Slippers*) for reading drafts, being polite enough to encourage me and in Matt's case, for pointing out an embarrassing number of errors and giving some priceless advice.

Finally, and most importantly, thanks and masses of love to Katy, Lucy and Todd for not thinking I'm a joke because, '*the stories that I told, I tell again and again!*' xxxx

Simon Shuttleworth
East Devon, May 2021.

Printed in Great Britain
by Amazon

64451585R00119